the treasury of
CATS

Contributors

Richard Patrick   Grace Pond FZS

Sir John Smyth VC   Christine Metcalf

Beverley Nichols   May Eustace

Octopus Books

Acknowledgements

The Publishers would like to thank the following individuals and organizations for their kind permission to reproduce the pictures in this book:—

B.P.C. 10
Bruce Coleman 8, 15, 18, 26, 27, 33, 75 right, 111 top right.
Rex Coleman 48, 56, 57.
Anne Cumbers 25, 28, 37, 38, 44–5, 47, 64, 65, 101, 103, 111 centre, 112 top left and centre, 117, 118–9, 120, 121, 126–7, 128, 129 top, 130, 131, 132, 133, 134, 135.
Dr Brian Eustace 68 top, 92, 93, 95.
Mary Evans Picture Library 14, 94.
Michael Holford 6, 9, 10, 11, 12.
Keystone Press Agency 30, 43, 49, 98.
John C. Madden 96.
Maine Coon Breeders Association 67.
The Mansell Collection 13, 16, 17.
Kenneth Miller 75.
Beverley Nichols 76, 79, 80, 81.
Octopus Books 51.
Popperfoto 7, 78, 84–5, 104.
Sir John Smyth VC 50–1, 52.
Spectrum Colour Library 20, 29, 30, 31, 34, 46, 54, 59, 62 top, 63, 66, 69, 73, 74, 88, 91, 97, 99, 105, 108, 109, 110, 112 bottom left, 116, 129.
Syndication International 22–3, 24, 25, 32, 35, 36, 40, 41, 52 bottom, 53, 55, 71, 77, 79, 82–3, 86–7, 111 top and bottom, 112, 113, 122–3, 124.
Sally Anne Thompson endpapers, 61, 62, 68 bottom, 70, 72, 98 top left and bottom, 106–7, 115, 125.

First published 1972 by
Octopus Books Limited,
59 Grosvenor Street, London W1

ISBN 7064 0008 9
© 1972 Octopus Books Limited
Reprinted 1975

Produced by Mandarin Publishers Limited
Toppan Building, Westlands Road,
Hong Kong

Printed in Hong Kong

Contents

Enter the cat

RICHARD PATRICK

Above, the Egyptians worshipped their cats and buried them with as much ceremony as humans – this is a mummified cat from Thebes.

Right, the cat's great cousin the lion has always been considered as king of the jungle.

Great Cats

It is an interesting fact that the cat – the domestic cat – is absent from classical mythology. Dogs and horses and birds abound; serpents and bulls, those ancient symbols of strength and fertility, are encountered at every turn – even monsters are invented to explain some half-understood fear. But the cat, the resourceful and graceful creature that could symbolize so much, is no part of our legacy from the ancient cultures.

The explanation is that the domestic cat is a newcomer, as time goes, to the company of man, and she is unique as the one and only animal that man took to himself for a non-utilitarian purpose. That she is the supreme enemy of small vermin is really an extra boon, a bonus that man earned by the way. She may well have taken to man because rats and mice were to be found wherever he dwelt – but that is a different story. Her independent nature and capacity for keeping her own counsel make her a very different pet from the slavishly adoring dog, and

one can be sure that the cat's acceptance of man is certainly on her own terms.

She joined him about 5,000 years ago, a miniature of the royal symbol of the lion which must be considered before we can understand how the cat walked into man's company and in a short space of time exacted veneration from him. She was a god before she ever became a pet.

The lion has been a symbol of power from the time that man first knew him. The creature was more widely distributed in ancient days; it was as familiar in western Asia as it is in tropical Africa now, and makes an appearance in the ancient tranditions of the Hindus. Appropriately, it symbolizes power; sometimes in divine form and sometimes in royal – it would be nearly impossible to draw a division between the two since kings in early cultures were usually the representatives of gods if not gods themselves. Western Asia and Egypt are regions where the sun can kill as easily as it can give life-stirring warmth, and in ancient

times it was feared and propitiated as much as it was invoked. The lion was the creature which symbolized solar heat.

The creature has almost vanished from India just as it has from western Asia, and its survival in Hindu tradition suggests that the migration of peoples which took the Aryans into India must, on the journey, have led them through the same sort of territory that their racial kindred, the Persians, made their home. The Hindu scriptures describe the deeds of the god Vishnu, and ascribe to him various appearances on earth when evil was abroad and man was suffering. One of these occasions saw the assumption of divine authority by a king who demanded that his subjects

and his family acknowledge him as a god. One of his sons refused, in spite of deprivation and, eventually, torture. The watchful god decided that it was time to make another appearance on earth – his fourth, according to the scriptures – to destroy the power of the evil king. He came to earth in the form of a lion.

– and small cats
It was in Egypt, lion country in ancient times, that the cat became a god and where she first entered the household. The history of this great empire of antiquity was of such duration that it encompassed a great range of beliefs. It also saw a constant shift of power from one region to another and the syncretization of

Above, a Caffre cat from which all domestic cats are said to be descended. Abyssinian cats closely resemble these majestic creatures.

Right, a bronze head and shoulders of the Egyptian lion goddess Sekhmet who later was represented as a cat.

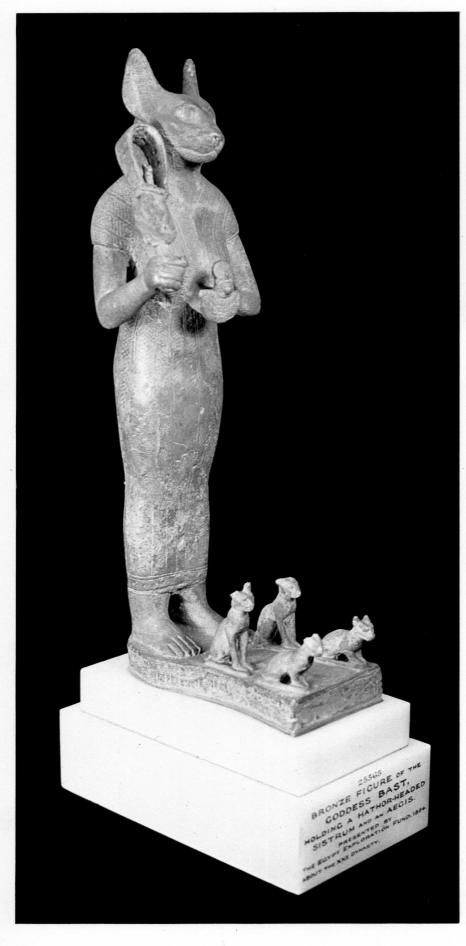

Above, a beautiful bronze cat called
the Gayer Anderson cat from the
British Museum.

Left, a bronze figure of the Goddess
Bast who was incarnate in all
living cats in Egypt, consequently
every domestic or stray cat was
regarded as sacred and the
Egyptians' veneration for them was
almost excessive.

Right, the Greeks did not bother
with small cats, but they admired
lions as is seen by the statues on
the Terrace of Lions at Delos,
the Greek Island.

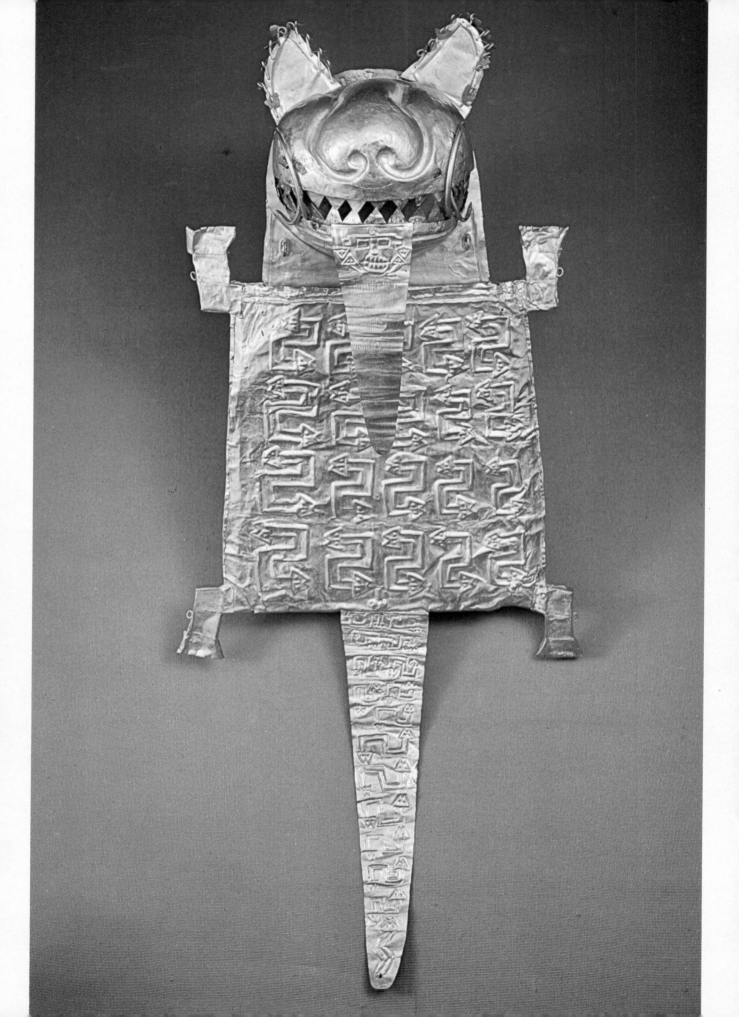

a fantastic number of local religions to form a faith acceptable to all. With the shift of power there was often a shift in fashionable religion – the ascendancy of Amon, the ram-headed god of Thebes, occurred when that city became the centre of power. An older city, Memphis, was where the lion as the symbol of solar light and brilliance found its chief expression about 5,000 years ago.

The creator god of Memphis was Ptah, represented by the bull: his consort was the lion-headed Sekhmet. Ptah generated life in a cow by his rays and his bull, the moon creature, represented fruition and growth. But the moon gives way to the sun, the ripener, which never waxes or wanes and which in spite of its benefits is to be feared. For this reason Sekhmet was called the Eye of Ra – she personified the sun god's destructive heat.

As we have seen, things were always changing in Egypt and though Ra, the sun god, endured he became Amon-Ra when the centre of power moved to Thebes about 3,500 years ago: Amon, the ascendant deity, took to himself the character of his rivals. The sun god still crossed the heavens during the day and still sank into the western horizon at night. He travelled, people said, in the solar barque, and before he could resume his journey over earth from the eastern horizon he had to pass through the dark regions below. His reappearance each morning was greeted with hymns of thankfulness.

One of the dangers faced was the great serpent Apep who waited eternally in the shades, hoping to destroy the sun on its journey, and a later tradition tells how the solar barque carried the Eye of Ra, who fought the serpent nightly, and

Left, a Peruvian gold puma mask of about 6th century A.D.

Top, a domestic scene from a Roman mosaic – cat catching a cock.

Right, a Siennese painting of a cat.

13

From one extreme to another; in the Western World cats were regarded as evil creatures and the many fifteenth century woodcuts of witches are full of fierce looking black cats.

people of the marshy region of the Nile Delta. Treated with respect, eventually with affection, she found her way into the temples, those man-made regions of coolness, and it wasn't long before the Egyptians, who made gods of every living creature, bestowed divine honours on the cat. A cult developed; the cat was acknowledged as the goddess Bast and her cult centre became the city called Bubastis. Sekhmet came to be regarded as one of the goddesses of olden times. The cat was cherished in the temples and there, when she died, she was embalmed and buried with full funerary honours. Anyone foolish enough to kill her paid for the crime with his life.

However, everything changes, even for divine cats. They became accustomed to the company of man and eventually entered his house. Condescending to domesticity, they carried with them a suggestion of sanctity and this led to a regard that even the most besotted cat-lover of today might think excessive. When the house cat died in ancient Egypt the whole household went into mourning; everyone cut off their hair and observed elaborate rites before embarking on the waiting period while another cat made up its mind to take possession of the empty place. To the Egyptians every cat was the same cat, so to speak; the goddess Bast incarnate.

The Western World
Having arrived, one might expect that the cat would have become a familiar part of the households of the ancient world. But, just as she is missing from Greek mythology, she is missing from the Greek people. We have evidence that she was *there*, and little more than that. And this is curious because the lion, her mighty cousin, was well known to the Greeks. He appears on Cretan seals and there is a celebrated survival, the Lion Gate of Mycenae, which may represent the ascendancy of the sun and sky gods who supplanted the cult of the Earth Mother; but the small cat seems to have meant nothing to them. They kept dogs, and had a charming habit of making cages for crickets and cicadas because they enjoyed their

nightly overcame it. But the Eye of Ra was no longer the fearsome, lion-headed Sekhmet. The Eye of Ra was now a cat. This was change indeed.

What had happened? The answer is obvious – puss had arrived on the scene and had taken over, as she always does.

From temple to threshold
A familiar creature in the Near East and Egypt was a feline species known as the Caffre cat, an animal a little larger than our house cat. The Caffre was regarded with favour because it preyed on, among other things, snakes and this was important to the

chirrupping. There is a reference to a cat in one of Aristophanes' plays, but the context suggests a wild cat, and a creature which *could* be a cat turns up on one or two Greek vases. That is all – no cat, no animal in fact, would ever have become a god for the Greeks.

The Romans were different. It is true that they used small snakes and weasels to kill mice so the appearance of the cat in Rome probably stems from two facts: they were the lords of Egypt and they were, especially the wealthy patricians, fascinated by novelty. Egyptian cults made a deep impression on them and it was inevitable that the pampered puss of the Egyptian household would find a similar place in Rome. As prolific then as she is now, the cat would soon have outgrown her place in wealthy households and been obliged to make do with the common people. Fifty years after the Battle of Actium the elder Pliny was referring to the cat as a well-known creature to be seen everywhere.

Hard times
Rome became mistress of the world, as we know. The centuries of her rule bestowed order on a large part of the world and where the Roman went the cat went too. There was another cat in the wild regions – but that one shunned the company of man. She kept company with the goddess Frigga of the Teutons and the wild cat was, and is, virtually untamable. Nevertheless the wild and domestic strains met and commingled and to this we owe much of the variety in size and colouring displayed by our domestic cats. In Western Europe under the Roman occupation 'The ordinary livestock of a villa included horses, cattle, sheep, and pigs; geese were often kept, and cats and dogs were, of course, indispensable'. (Collingwood and Myers: *Roman Britain and the English Settlements*)

The statement is fascinating, not least because it is so positive. Unfortunately the Pax Romana did not endure; in the fifth century AD the Romans abandoned their conquests and departed to try to meet the danger threatening the Eternal City. Western Europe was left to undergo a nightmare of violence and destruc-

tion and when some degree of order and civilization returned it was to a world so crippled in the soul that the lighter, more graceful side of Graeco-Roman culture lay buried until the Renaissance, nine centuries later.

This was to prove hard on the cat. The very qualities that had made her welcome to civilized man – her beauty, her grace, her independent nature, her nocturnal pleasures, her seeking the company of those who made least demands on her and gave her the most comfort in return – old and lonely people – were to make her an object of suspicion

A typical wild cat from Scotland. In spite of looking as docile as a domestic cat, these creatures are virtually impossible to tame and keep themselves to themselves.

in a fear-riddled and superstitious society. When once the cat became associated in the minds of stupid people with the idea of witchcraft, the poor creature was to endure unspeakable treatment at the hands of men. No sensible person believes such things now and we can be thankful for that, though we have little reason for self-congratulation in the matter of our relations with domestic pets.

There was another reason for Western man's attitude to the cat in medieval times. Where the torments of hell were promised to anyone who departed from the church's ruling, and where this rule had lately replaced paganism – which was in most of Europe – the memory of the old beliefs was strong. It would not have been long before that the people of the northern plains had known the cat as the corn-spirit, and dissuaded their children from molesting the growing corn by telling them that the corn-cat lived there; that in many parts of Gaul the last sheaf of corn was called the cat's tail, and that before the reaping commenced a cat was garlanded with flowers and ribbons; that in Silesia the reaper who cut the last sheaf was called Tom-cat and given a pointed tail to wear; that in Picardy a cat was offered as a sacrifice when the harvest was gathered in. These were the old beliefs and, said the churchmen, the old beliefs were the devil's work. It must follow that the cat was the devil's creature, and would only consort with those who served him.

The church, anxious and insecure, gave no quarter to those who made the slightest departure from the rules, and for centuries the charge of heresy against a person, or a community, could result in ruthless and bloody persecution. It was an age when charity seemed to have departed completely from the men of God.

It has to be acknowledged that heretical movements were frequent in Europe in the early Middle Ages – centuries were to pass before the power of Rome succeeded in quelling the mere thought of a different belief. The statements made at heresy trials are, at this distance of time, quite staggeringly idiotic; but they were believed, and thousands

of men and women died because of them. Again and again there is mention in them of a cat, usually as the devil himself. It was said of the Cathars that they held secret conventicles in which the devil was worshipped in the form of a cat. Gregory IX, the pope who founded the Inquisition, gave instruction to the Archbishop of Mainz to preach against heresy in Germany. The pope knew, apparently, exactly how heretics were initiated – one might wonder *how* he knew. He told the Archbishop that the heretics sat down to a communal meal, and, before giving themselves over to abominable lusts, received among themselves a black tom-cat. The novice was fully received only after he had kissed the tom-cat under the tail. The cat turns up in the trials of the Luciferans at Marburg, and in those of the Knights Templars in France.

It went very hard for puss that she had ever been designated the corn spirit in the old religion. Her presence – when the heretical movements had been crushed and the Inquisition had time for smaller game – was to bring the scales down against the survival of many people who were isolated, or withdrawn, or simply the victim of someone's spite.

But society then, as now, moved

on several levels. The poor had no one to speak for them and the rich, as always, did much as they liked and had no hesitation in deciding what was good for others. The first witchcraft trials took place in Europe in the thirteenth century but there is ample evidence that the kings and nobles, while agreeing that cats and witches must be burned together, did nothing to keep the cats away from their palaces. The monasteries always kept cats, for the simple reason that the cat was, in spite of the lunatic convictions that overcame

Right, this programme cover from Drury Lane Theatre shows the popular pantomine character Dick Whittington with his cat.

Below, an illustration from Boswell's 'Life of Johnson' showing the famous cat Hodge asleep at his master's feet.

Drawn by H. Corbould.   Engraved by E. Finden.

D. H. FRISTON

the churchmen at witchcraft trials, the main defence of people everywhere against vermin. It might be wondered how a single cat could have survived the madder seasons; but puss is a nimble creature and good at taking care of herself. She survived. When the universal church and the Inquisition had passed from the earth she was still there, ready to sit with man – if she felt like it.

But her reputation for strangeness did not depart quickly. The last trial for witchcraft took place in England in 1712, the last in Scotland in 1722; in both a cat was named as the witch's familiar. Cardinal Wolsey, the most powerful and probably the most hated man in England for 15 years, took his cat to the dinner table, to audiences – to the cathedral itself when he was officiating at services. Richelieu, more powerful even than Wolsey, loved cats and gave orders that they be maintained at court. Hated as much as Wolsey, his predilection must have suggested something· sinister to his enemies·in that superstitious age. The Cardinal made ample provision for his cats – 14 of them – in his will; but he was no sooner dead than his Swiss guards rounded up the poor creatures and burned them.

In spite of all this puss had managed to enter European legend. Every child now knows the story of Dick Whittington and his marvellous cat, and Perrault immortalized his French counterpart when he wrote down and gave literary form to the old story of *Le maître chat ou le chat botté*, known to the English-speaking world as *Puss in Boots*. And reason eventually prevailed; with the morbid fear of witchcraft gone man and cat settled down together. Hodge, Samuel Johnson's much-loved cat, was famous among his wide circle of friends, and thereafter the cat is found to be the valued friend of writers everywhere. Not a Blue Persian, or an Abyssinian, or a Seal Point Siamese – what sort of cat is rarely mentioned. Probably they were just ordinary cats, as pretty and graceful and affectionate as even the most ordinary cat can be.

The New World

In ancient America the cats, great and small, had an honoured place. In Mexico there was a guild of Aztec knights whom the Spanish chroniclers called the Knights Tiger – the creature which they called the tiger being the small, beautiful ocelot. The knights were not warriors but initiates in a mystical order striving for illumination. The ocelot was the creature that called a greeting to the sun – they could hear it at every dawn – and it was the sun that ruled their lives. The ocelot was the animal of the Fifth Sun, the age in which the Aztecs were living at the time of the Conquest. The age before that, the Fourth Sun, was that of the jaguar and scholars believe, on the evidence of the precious and elusive jaguar masks, that there was in earlier times a powerful jaguar cult.

In South America the traces are ubiquitous but the records existed only verbally; the destruction of the high Andean civilization by the Spaniards destroyed all hope of our ever learning the true details of the Andean way of life – what the recurring feline images can have meant we can only guess. Jaguars and pumas can be seen on pottery, in carvings, woven into the exquisite textiles, beaten into gold. That the great cats were cult animals seems certain but that is all that can be said. It is not surprising that they were, since they are beyond question the most majestic and beautiful creatures of the New World.

The small cats of America, the ocelots and margays, are exquisite creatures, not much bigger than our domestic cats and with markings in their warm brown – almost magenta-coloured – fur that make a striking effect. They are easily tamed and playful and one can imagine them gracing the homes of the Aztec and Inca families. We will never know if they did.

Now they are becoming popular as pets and it may be that puss, the queen of every household she enters, is due for yet more strains to add to her present colours and sizes. That she herself will never really change her nature we can be quite sure, and every cat-lover will be glad of it.

A beautiful ocelot from America where they are now becoming increasingly popular as pets.

The domestic pet

GRACE POND FZS

To many people a cat is just a small furry animal useful for catching rats and mice, and that is all. To others it is a member of the household and a charming and decorative companion. There are also those who have never owned a cat in their lives but, because of changed circumstances, loneliness, or perhaps a move to a house with a garden, consider having one but hesitate as they know so little about the attention needed. It is with these people in mind that this chapter is written.

It is as well to weigh up carefully the advantages and disadvantages of ownership before taking on any animal. It should be remembered that a kitten is a living creature, a responsibility needing constant care and regular feeding. He will have to be house-trained, with litter trays changed frequently, and his food will have to be prepared and given at

All cats make loveable pets whether they are pedigree show cats or just an ordinary short-hair like this smiling white cat. A collar and a name tag are always a good idea.

regular hours. He will require grooming and, above all, time must be found to play with him and show him affection. At holiday times, even if he is only to be left for a day or so, arrangements will have to be made for his welfare; young kittens cannot be left on their own for many hours, and adult cats too need companionship. If you are out at work all day but still feel you cannot live without a kitten, a happy solution is to have two so they will be company for each other. Even then, kittens need to be fed several times a day and it may be possible for a neighbour to come in and give the mid-day meal and check that all is well.

These then are the disadvantages, although most owners do not regard them as such, finding pleasure in looking after their pets.

The advantages are many. Cats do not need to be taken out for exercise although they can be trained to walk on a lead if so desired. Being small in size they are not big eaters and if neutered they are quiet, unobtrusive and affectionate companions and, what is more, are always there to come home to.

A rest in the sun for this pensive tabby who has made himself comfortable as only a cat can on top of an asbestos roof.

Cats appreciate a garden, but many live happily in apartments and get sufficient exercise from chasing a ball around. They all love sleeping in the sun and if there is a small balcony suitable for this it should be wired in, if high up, as cats do not always land on their feet as commonly supposed, and a fall from a height may result in death or a broken limb. If there is no balcony, a small wire frame could be made to fit the window exactly, so that it may be left open in suitable weather.

Barring accidents cats live a long time, 13 or 14 years being the average, but 20 or even more not being unknown, so if you decide to take on the responsibility of a kitten, choose with care and make sure that you get what you really want.

Should money be a consideration, mongrel kittens are very inexpensive; but if you yearn for a decorative Siamese, a square Short-haired British or Exotic, or an aristocratic Persian, the price will be very much more.

Unless breeding is being considered there is really no necessity to be dogmatic as to the sex of the kitten. Neutering is fairly simple these days and castrating a male costs comparatively little, while the spaying of a female is rather more expensive. Nevertheless some animal welfare societies are prepared to help towards the cost of spaying if it is more than can be afforded.

If wishing to determine the sex of a kitten, the easiest way is to hold it in the hand and look under the tail.

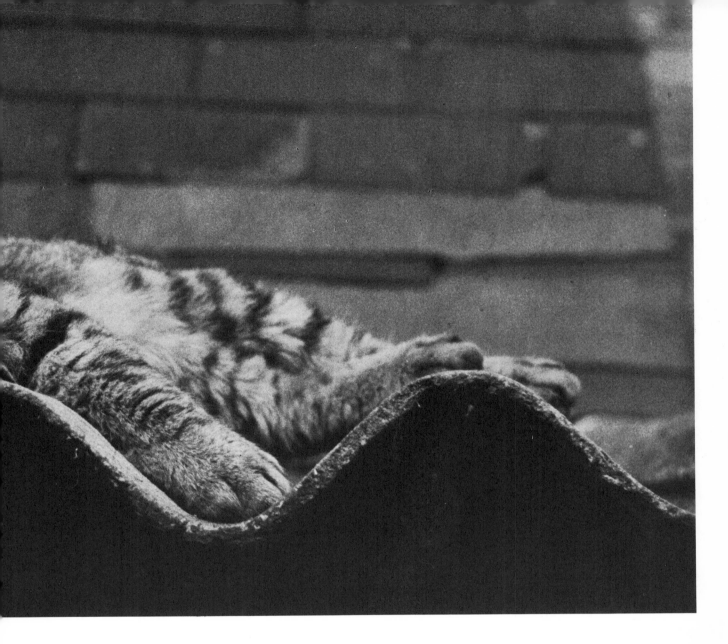

A male kitten has a circular anus near the base of the tail, with rudimentary testicles about half an inch away, while the female has a circular anus with a small slit, the entrance to the vagina, positioned very close to the anus under the tail. If there are both sexes in a litter, sexing is more easily done by comparison.

It is far better for kittens that are to be kept purely as pets to be altered or neutered. An entire male will certainly be most affectionate when he is at home, but as he reaches maturity, he will want to follow his natural instincts and call on all the female cats in the district or even further afield, probably coming home battle-scarred and starving. If kept in the house he will spray on the walls and curtains, leaving his strong and unpleasant odour everywhere.

A female will start calling, or be on heat, or come into season, at any age from about five months. The first heat is unmistakable with most females. She will tread up and down on the ground with her back legs, making loud howling noises, and be even more affectionate than usual. She may try to get out to look for a mate, and visiting males will certainly soon be waiting hopefully around outside. Should she succeed in finding a male, the gestation period is approximately 65 days.

The recommended age for altering or spaying is about three and a half months for a male and four and a half for a female, dependent on development. These ages apply to Britain. In the United States it is suggested that after the first heat is better for the female and at about eight months for the male, but professional advice should be sought as to the best time for a particular kitten.

It may not always be easy to find a kitten when wanted. With so many female cats being spayed, mongrel kittens are not as plentiful as they used to be, which is a very good thing as there are less strays. They may be advertised in local newspapers or on advertisement boards outside pet shops, or be given away by friends only too eager to find good homes. The animal welfare societies in many countries are usually looking for suitable homes

for unwanted cats and kittens.

If you prefer a pedigree kitten it is a good idea to visit a cat show, see what the various breeds look like, and possibly order one while there. *Fur and Feather* (Idle, Bradford, Yorks), a weekly periodical, and *Cats* (66, The Dale, Widley, Portsmouth), a bi-monthly magazine, in Britain; *Cats* (Washington, Pa) and *International Cat Fancy* (641, Lexington Avenue, New York), in the United States carry advertisements for pedigree cats and kittens.

Before buying a kitten visit, if possible, the home where he was born and see the conditions under which he has been raised, making sure that both mother and kittens look happy and healthy. The kitten you finally choose should be at least nine to ten weeks old, with a full set of milk teeth, fully weaned, used to a small variety of food, and house-trained. He should be gay and lively, steady on his legs, able to run

freely, with little tail held high. His eyes should be wide open, bright and sparkling, and inside the ears should be quite clean, with no smell or discharge. The nose should be cool to the touch and not running. There should be no signs of diarrhoea under the tail, nor should there be any flea dirts, looking like black specks, in the coat. The fur should be springy to the touch, not lank and clinging. If buying a pedigree kitten as a pet, it will not matter if the ears are too big (if a Persian) or too small (if a Siamese), as a perfect show specimen is really only important from a breeding or exhibiting point of view, and such small faults will in no way detract from the appearance or the charm of the kitten. It is essential that he should be inoculated against Feline Infectious Enteritis, and if not already done by the breeder this should be attended to as soon as the kitten has settled in; until then he

A Chartreux cat from Belgium expressing his opinion of England . . . laughter, boredom, or just a measured opinion? These cats are very like the British Blue in shape and colour.

Top right, kittens' traditional plaything . . . note the very clear 'M' marking on their foreheads which is typical of good tabbies.

Bottom right, the new arrival, not much more than a ball of fluff.

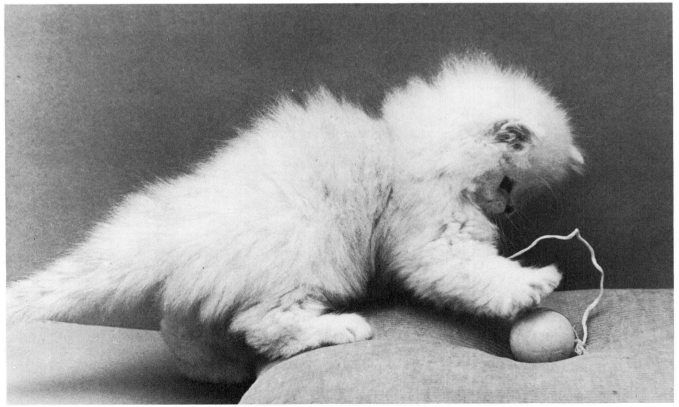

should be kept indoors and away from other cats.

It is not necessary to buy expensive equipment for your pet. There are some very good cat baskets available, but most kittens sleep perfectly happily in a low cardboard or wooden box with a blanket and newspaper in the bottom. It should be placed in a corner well away from draughts and raised slightly from the floor.

Whether pedigree or mongrel, all cats need some grooming and should have their own small soft brush and suitable combs. Some playthings such as a small ball or rubber mouse should be provided.

A kitten should never be bought as a pet for a very small child. It is difficult for a mother to keep a constant watch to see that there is no mishandling, and as the bones of a kitten are very fragile they are easily bent or broken by hugging and squeezing, and the tail may be broken by pulling.

On arriving at his new home the kitten should be put in a room with the windows closed and the fireplace and chimney covered, as in these days of central heating he may never have seen a fire and may consider the chimney a means of escape – with disastrous results! A litter tray should be ready, as he may need to use it after his journey. There are some excellent plastic litter trays available, but an oven pan will do just as well. It should be low enough for the kitten to get into and out of with ease, and should be filled with earth, or a proprietary cat litter, ashes, peat moss, or even torn-up newspaper. It is advisable to change the contents frequently as cats are fastidious animals, refusing to use smelly trays. It should always be kept in the same spot, so that the kitten knows where to go. If a garden is available, he could be taken out there under guard once he has settled in.

When he first arrives he may be

Above, a delicious, back-scratching roll on some gravel, and to complete the ecstacy? A toy mouse stuffed with catmint under one ear.

Right, a Shetland sheepdog puppy and tabby kitten make friends.

nervous and a little miserable in strange surroundings, missing his mother and little brothers and sisters. He should be allowed to wander around the room as he pleases, and should not be fussed over unduly. If there is a dog or another cat in the house, they should not be left alone together for the first few days, until it is clear that they are really friendly. Patience may be needed to achieve this, and to avoid jealousy care must be taken not to make too much of the new arrival in front of the older pets.

If there is a child in the house he must be taught that a small kitten needs plenty of sleep, and also that the kitten should not be regarded as a toy to be picked up and pulled about willy-nilly. The child should be shown the correct way to hold the kitten, with one hand under and around the back and the other under the chest. A kitten must never be picked up by the back of the neck, as this may damage the muscles. Mother cats only carry their kittens this way when very small.

If the kitten has come from a breeder, the diet sheet provided should be adhered to closely for the first few days, and any new items should be introduced gradually. Milk should only be given very sparingly, if at all. Some kittens, particularly Siamese, are quite unable to tolerate milk and suffer from diarrhoea if given it to drink. If there are no ill-effects it can be included in the diet, but it is a food, not a drink, and clean water should always be available instead.

A kitten of nine or ten weeks requires four or five small meals a day at regular times. Starting with a tablespoonful at each meal, the amounts may be increased slightly each week, and the number of meals cut down, until at the age of six or seven months he is having three meals a day. By the time he is nine months old, two meals a day should be sufficient.

Cats are carnivorous or flesh eaters, and meat, especially raw, is an essential feature of the diet. Fish is not, but some should be included to provide variety. Too much fish, or a diet of fish alone, may produce a form of eczema.

All food given to small kittens should be cut up small or minced, as they can choke on large chunks.

The following may be included in the diet:
Beef (*raw or cooked*)
Rabbit (*cooked*)
Chicken (*cooked*)
Lamb (*cooked*)
Heart (*raw or cooked*). Only as part of a mixed diet, as too much may cause a mineral deficiency.
Horsemeat (*cooked or raw*). Only that offered for human consumption.
Liver (*cooked or raw*). Too much raw liver may cause diarrhoea.
Kidneys (*cooked or raw*)
Tongues (*cooked*)
Veal (*cooked*)
Any cooked white fish with bones removed.
Strained baby foods
Baby cereals
Tinned pilchards
Tinned salmon
Tinned sardines
Tinned herrings
Cooked vegetables such as peas, beans or carrots may be added to the meal if liked. A few cornflakes or a similar cereal, or brown bread, should be added to provide roughage. Cows' or tinned milk can be given if tolerated. Canned cat foods

are a good standby and it is as well to include some in the diet so that the cat is used to them; but they should not be given to very young kittens as they can be too rich.

A large raw beef bone may be given especially to help when teething, but cooked bones should never be given to any cat or kitten. Chicken and rabbit bones cooked or raw should always be avoided as they can splinter and cause internal injuries. A few drops of a vitamin

oil should be added to the food daily during the winter. Uneaten food should never be left down, particularly in the summer, as it can become stale or fly-infested and cause gastric enteritis.

Grass is a natural emetic and should always be available as it helps the cat bring up any hair swallowed, preventing furball. If there is no garden, grass can be grown indoors quite easily in a pot.

As cats always seem to be washing

themselves it is frequently not realized that grooming is necessary as well to rid the coat of dust and dirt and any loose hairs that may be licked down and could cause furball.

It is as well to start the grooming the day after the kitten arrives so that he becomes used to being handled, and if played with for a short time afterwards the grooming period will soon be looked forward to with pleasure. A fairly soft bristle

28

Tabbies . . . and opposite, a proud black Mum with irresistible grey kittens which are rapidly growing too big for their basket.

Above, 'eating is a serious business for a growing kitten like me, and I am not sure if I like this new food yet'.

Left, Siamese cats are expert at finding a warm place to sit where they will also receive as much admiration as possible.

brush, not a wire one, and two steel combs will be necessary, one with very fine teeth to catch any odd flea that may be picked up, and one with wider teeth for daily combing. Naturally a long-coated cat will need more attention than one with short fur, but the general procedure is the same. First feel through the coat to make sure there are no prickles or burrs in the fur, and tease out any tangles with the fingers. Comb and brush all over, placing the kitten flat on his back in your lap to do the stomach. Finish with hard hand stroking if you have a short-haired kitten, or with brushing up the fur, particularly round the face, if you have a long-haired kitten. Any dirt in the corner of the eyes should be wiped away gently with cotton wool, as should any dust in the ears. If the coat is neglected, and bad matts and tangles form, it may be necessary

to cut these away with round-ended scissors, taking care not to pull or cut the skin. The cat's appearance will suffer for a while but the fur will soon grow again.

Training should start as soon as the kitten has settled down. Most kittens soon learn to use their litter trays, and if there is an occasional accident he should never be smacked but shown the spot, spoken to sharply and taken and put on the tray. If there is a garden that he is able to go in, he should at first be taken out under escort, but very soon he will be able to go out alone. If he has been using a litter tray it could be moved a little nearer the door each day, eventually being placed outside and then removed altogether when he uses the garden. Unfortunately some cats become so used to having a tray that they come in from the garden to use it.

As previously remarked, the con-

tents must be changed frequently, as should it begin to smell or become unduly wet, it will be disdained by the cat.

The kitten should never be allowed to claw on the furniture and any attempt to do so should be stopped immediately. A sharp 'No' is better than smacking, as the animal will not realize it is a punishment and will just think he is being cruelly treated. The kitten should be shown where he is allowed to claw, and if there is no garden with a tree most pet shops sell special scratching posts for this purpose. Alternatively a large log, or string wound round the leg of the kitchen table, will be quite suitable.

It is sometimes an advantage to have your cat used to a lead, and training for this should start when the kitten is about three months old. Most pet shops or animal welfare societies sell elastic collars and suitable leads which are better for young kittens, although harnesses can be used when the cat is fully grown. Patience will be needed and also plenty of time, with the collar and lead being put on for a few minutes only for the first few days until the kitten is used to it. The first time walking on a lead is attempted the kitten will probably sit down and refuse to move, but eventually he will get the idea and will walk a few steps. Increase the distance slightly each day until, by the end of a few weeks, you will be able to take him

Above, a Burmese cat having a thorough clean between the claws – which is what this greedy chap (right) is going to need by the time he has finished the tin. Most cats will eat with their paws if the container is too small and their whiskers touch the sides.

34

out with you for short walks.

A lead is useful if you wish to take your pet in the car with you, as no cat should be allowed complete freedom then. Accidents have been caused this way before now, with the cat jumping unexpectedly on to the back of his owner, or getting under his feet when the brakes are being applied.

Most cats can be trained to do a few simple tricks, although being such independent creatures will not always do them to order but only when they feel like it. Many will retrieve paper balls thrown for them time and time again, with their owners tiring before they do. Some enjoy hide and seek and will search for a small hidden toy, while others hide away, pouncing on their owners with glee as they walk by. They teach themselves to beg, open cupboards and refrigerators, turn on taps and open doors. They can be very affectionate, putting both paws round their owners' necks and licking their faces. Being highly intelligent, sensitive animals, they dislike being laughed at, scolded or shouted at, and will sulk if offended. Pleasure is expressed by purring, padding up and down with the paws (known as 'kneading the dough') and closing the eyes as if smiling when spoken to.

A few general remarks regarding travel may be helpful here. It is not generally realized that to prevent the introduction of rabies cats do

A pole covered with carpeting makes a good scratching post.

Right, one of the rare, curly-coated Rex cats shows that 'walking the cat' in a harness and lead is as much fun as 'walking the dog'.

not have freedom of movement into and out of Britain, although this does not apply to the United States. Any cat leaving Britain and then returning has to spend a period of six months in strict isolation in a quarantine cattery.

In Britain cats are allowed in containers on buses and coaches only at the conductor's discretion. On trains they may travel accompanied or unaccompanied, but must again be in an adequate container.

If unable to take your pet with you on holiday it may be necessary to find a good boarding cattery to take him to. Make an inspection of the cattery before booking and see the actual house and run your pet will occupy. Most catteries are excellent but there are some poor ones. It may be necessary to book up months in advance, so do not leave it too late. You will probably be asked to supply a certificate stating that your cat has been inoculated against Feline Infectious Enteritis, and you may also have to supply a vet's certificate stating that the animal is in good health.

Owning a cat not only means seeing that he has a good varied diet, daily grooming and plenty of affection without being pampered, but also means making sure that he is fit. Fortunately the majority of cats are healthy animals, and barring accidents rarely need the services of a vet. Living in close association with a cat should enable the owner to detect very quickly when all is not well. Cats go down so rapidly that it is false economy to doctor your pet yourself, when possibly immediate treatment with antibiotics may mean the difference between life and death. It is important to telephone the vet at once with brief

details of the cat's symptoms, and he will advise. If it comes to nothing no harm has been done, but you may have cut the length of the illness considerably by early treatment should something serious be developing. If cost has to be considered, many of the animal welfare societies run animal clinics.

There are two major illnesses which affect kittens and cats. One is Feline Infectious Enteritis or Panleucopenia, which is a killer, invariably proving fatal once it has been contracted. It need not be, as inoculations are available which give practically one hundred per cent protection. Several vaccines are available, usually given in the form of two injections, but your vet will advise as to the best one, and the right age at which it should be given, usually when the kitten is about 10 weeks old.

Feline Infectious Enteritis can kill in a matter of hours, with poison being blamed rather than an illness. The symptoms are generally a high fever, loss of appetite, slight vomiting, general lassitude and dehydration. The kitten may sit with his head over a bowl of water without drinking, or may crouch in a dark corner disinterested in anything. The vet should be called in at once as minutes count at the onset of this illness and the only hope is immediate treatment.

The virus is so violent that no new kitten should be introduced into a home where this illness has been present until at least six months afterwards, and then he should have been inoculated at least three or four weeks before. The premises should have been thoroughly disinfected, and the cat's blankets, basket, toys and so on destroyed. All contact with other cats and cat owners should be avoided, even to the extent of not writing letters from an infected household.

The other mo t serious illness is Pneumonitis, also known as cat flu' or distemper. It can cause death but does respond to early treatment with antibiotics. The symptoms are running eyes and nose, sneezing, wheezing, possibly diarrhoea, high temperature, and refusal of food. There are a number of illnesses of a similar respiratory nature under this heading and the symptoms may vary. The illness may be long and recovery slow, but careful nursing and a nourishing diet should effect a complete cure. If necessary, the animal may have to be given injections and be force-fed to keep him alive. A small quantity of glucose dissolved in warm water and given in the side of the mouth with a medicine dropper may help to keep him going.

Some vets do vaccinate against Pneumonitis, but as the illness is known in so many forms it may be difficult to find the correct antidote.

Nursing is important in all cases of cat illness, as they become very depressed and will give up easily. The patient should be isolated in a warm but not overheated room, and given a cardboard box lined with old blankets to sleep on, all of which should be destroyed when the cat has recovered. He must not be left alone for long hours but visited frequently, and talked to cheerfully, as cats sense atmosphere very quickly. The owner should wear an overall when going into the room, changing his shoes and washing his hands afterwards. To make the cat feel more comfortable any mucus from the nose should be wiped away, and the areas around the mouth and under the tail washed with slightly dampened cotton wool.

Once the patient begins to recover he should be tempted with tiny morsels of his favourite food.

Cats can be taught to do simple tricks, but they won't just perform them at the word of the command, only if they feel like it and preferably if there is an audience.

Left, some cats don't like milk, others love it so much that they are expert at stealing the best of the milk every morning.

Right, opening a shut door is no problem at all . . . while Tibs the Tomcat has learnt to ring his own door bell installed specially for him.

It may be necessary to push a little into his mouth so that he gets the taste. In some illnesses the sense of smell may be lost so something with a strong flavour, such as tinned pilchards, should be tried at first; anything to get him to start eating again of his own accord.

There are various contingencies which may occur during a cat's lifetime, as follows:

Abscess

An abscess may develop after a fight with another cat, and is caused by a puncture of the skin that is so small that it passes unnoticed until the cat looks miserable and goes off his food. Close examination will reveal a hard shining swelling, which gradually grows larger. This is filled with pus and may have to be brought

to a head with thrice-daily hot water fomentations – hot but not boiling. Professional treatment is recommended as the vet may consider antibiotic injections necessary. The fur should be cut short around the swelling, and lancing may be needed with a sterilized needle when the swelling has come to a head. Once the pus is out the cat will be in much less pain and should start eating. The wound should not be allowed to close up too quickly as the abscess may possibly redevelop.

Bites
During a fight with another, a cat may be bitten, and any such wound should be bathed with a mild disinfectant to prevent sepsis.

Broken bones
A bone may be broken should a cat be hit by a car, receive a blow, or fall from a height breaking a limb. If this is suspected, keep the cat warm and as still as possible, calling in the vet immediately.

Constipation
This may occur due to change of diet when the kitten goes to his new home, or otherwise may be due to too dry feeding or underfeeding. A small teaspoonful of corn or mineral oil may effect a cure, but if persistent, professional advice must be sought as it may be caused by a furball or a blockage.

Diarrhoea

This may happen with a change of home, and may be due to excess of milk, wrong or too wet feeding. In the summer, a frequent cause is fly-infected food. All food should be withheld and water only given to drink, and if the condition continues for more than a day the vet should be consulted, as it may be the start of severe illness.

Ear troubles

Sitting with the head on one side, pawing at the ears, or shaking the head may be the first indication of ear trouble. Close inspection may show a dark brown discharge, with an unpleasant smell, indicating the presence of ear mites, generally referred to as canker. As there are various types a vet should be consulted to prescribe the correct treatment.

Eye troubles

Some cats with very short noses have a brown discharge in the corners of the eyes which should be wiped away daily so that the face is not permanently stained.

Severe inflammation with a sticky discharge and pawing at the eye by the cat may be conjunctivitis, which is contagious and should be treated professionally.

Fleas

Many cats pick up an occasional flea, but should never be allowed to become infested, as having fleas and tape worms go together. The daily grooming should ensure that any odd flea is discovered, but should the fur be full of tiny black specks, which are the dirts, a suitable insecticide must be used with care, following the procedure given on the container. No insecticides of any kind should be used on young kittens or nursing mothers, even if advocated as safe, as any powder licked down can cause the death of small animals.

Poisoning

A cat may become fatally ill through licking or swallowing substances which are poisonous to them, such as weed-killers or flea powders containing D.D.T. or eating rats that have been poisoned. Aspirin should never be given to a cat as this also is a poison. As treatment depends entirely on the type of poisoning, the symptoms should be telephoned to the vet immediately. In an emergency a piece of washing soda pushed down the cat's throat, or making him drink some salt water, may induce sickness thereby saving his life.

Skin troubles

There are several skin complaints from which a cat may suffer. These include eczema, which is frequently caused by an allergy, mange, and ringworm, both the latter being contagious. Any bare patches in the fur, particularly round ones, should be suspect and veterinary treatment is essential.

Stings

Although the fur usually gives adequate protection, cats may be stung through patting at a bee or a wasp. If possible pull out the sting, dabbing the place with a mild disinfectant. A sting in the mouth and throat with much swelling must be treated as serious, necessitating urgent veterinary treatment.

Teething

At about the age of five or six months the second teeth begin to appear, and the milk teeth fall out. The kitten may go off his food and on examination it will be seen that his gums are inflamed. A daily dose of milk of magnesia and easily eaten food should be given. He may have to be encouraged to eat with tiny pieces of his favourite food.

In an older cat dribbling or bad breath may be the sign of bad teeth or tarter, both of which can easily be dealt with by the vet.

Worms

Worms in cats and kittens cause debility and loss of weight, even anaemia. Round worms are not quite as serious as tape, but neither should be allowed to persist. Not all kittens do suffer from worms and it is not necessary to worm as a matter of course, but if they are suspected the vet should be asked to prescribe the correct tablets for the size, weight, and age of the animal, as indiscriminate worming-out has caused the death of many small animals.

Round worms

A kitten with worms may have a coat that looks in poor condition, with a swollen belly and bad breath. Worms may be vomited or seen in the motions, like thin pieces of string. Round worms are far more serious in kittens than adults.

Tape worm

If a cat has a large appetite but still looks thin and in poor condition, a tape worm should be suspected. This is serious, causing anaemia, debility, even fits. Segments of the flat worm may be seen hanging from the cat's anus or sticking to his fur like dried segments of rice grains. Fleas act as the intermediary host to the tapeworm, so if there are fleas in his coat a cat may also suffer from a tapeworm. As the head attaches itself to the intestines, with the body growing up to several feet in length, it is essential that the correct medicine prescribed by the vet is given to ensure that the whole worm is expelled without doing internal damage. After treatment, it may be necessary to give extra raw meat to counteract anaemia.

The foregoing are the minor ailments which *may* affect your pet – but fortunately rarely do, as apart from inoculations and neutering many cats never have to visit a vet in their lives.

The way your cat's personality develops will depend on you and on his upbringing, and although to you he may seem almost human it should be remembered that the cat is a domestic animal and as such should be allowed to live as far as possible a life of his own, without pampering or undue fuss. Treated and fed correctly, you will have the pleasure of his company for many a long year.

The residents of this cats' home are not at all put out by the appearance of a large and hairy theatre cat – food is much more important.

Siamese

SIR JOHN SMYTH VC

Above, an intelligent and inquisitive Seal Point kitten determined to have its own way.

Opposite, a Lilac or 'Frost' Point Siamese Queen – she is lighter in colour than the Chocolate Point but darker than the Blue Point.

Previous page, a Chocolate Point champion Siamese.

I suppose a Siamese kitten is one of the most beautiful little animals in the world; its colouring, its enormous blue eyes and its lively and charming manners cannot fail to enchant. But to the true cat fan it is the adult cat which makes the most appeal, and the grace, intelligence, personality and character of the Siamese, together with its friendly nature and love of humans, make it one of the most attractive of all breeds of cat.

What is a Siamese? The term is applied generically to cats which have what are known as 'points', or, in other words, have coloured ears, feet, tails and masks. Today there are several different coloured points which are accepted for breeding and show purposes by the Governing Council of the Cat Fancy.

Many legends surround its origin. A popular belief is that the breed is descended from the Palace cats of Siam, the first of which is said to have been imported into Britain in 1884, as a present from the King of Siam to the British Consul-General in Bangkok, Mr Owen Gould. This cat was exhibited at the Crystal Palace Show of 1885 by his sister, Mrs Veley. About 1886 she obtained a pair and two kittens from Bangkok and brought them back to England. In the same year Miss Forestier-Walker obtained one male and three females. In 1892 the first standard of points was published in *Our Cats*. So the cats imported between 1884 and 1887 formed the foundation stock for most of the Siamese bred in Britain.

The origin of the Siamese in America presents a conflicting picture, many different people being cited as the first Siamese owners. But the first Siamese to win a Best Cat award (at the Michigan Cat Club, Detroit, in 1907) was Loch-

aven Siam. From this time on the Siamese grew in popularity in the States, though in those early days the breed was delicate and the kitten population grew slowly. However, information on the breeding, rearing and care of Siamese was obtained from Britain, where more success had been achieved in the first years. The quest for the secret of strong, healthy Siamese culminated with the founding of the Siamese Cat Club of America in April, 1909; and from then onwards the breed went from strength to strength. In 1925 the first Siamese Specialty Show in America took place in Detroit, and in 1946 a National Siamese Cat Club was founded. There are of course many other Siamese Cat Clubs in America, where the Siamese is now the most popular breed.

In those early days the breed was predominantly of one kind, the Seal Point, although Blue Points, Chocolate Points and Lilac Points did appear from time to time; but these were considered to be 'sports'. The Seal Points are characterized by a cream body colour, shading to pale, warm fawn on the back, with mask, ears, legs, feet and tail of dark brown, with no pale hairs. However, this characteristic Siamese colouring is not unique to Siamese cats, some people claiming that it appeared in the near extinct hairless cat of Mexico and among other animals such as rabbits, mice, sheep and cattle, and that it is therefore a widely dispersed coat pattern. Others claim that Siamese type cats were seen in Europe and America long before 1884 and that painters of various nationalities have portrayed them. As ships' cats travelled to many ports it would not be surprising if Siamese types appeared in many places long before 1884.

But as they were not shown in cat shows prior to 1886 no one took any special note and they were probably just referred to as 'that quaint coloured cat'.

In recent years certain other colour points have appeared through experimental breeding, variously described as Red Points, Tabby-points, Tortie Points and even Cream Points, which are all accepted as recognized variations in this country for show purposes, but which are in a separate breed class (Class 32) by reason of the fact that they are 'manufactured' colourings. But the general body shape has remained constant.

Siamese should have long, svelte bodies, with thin legs, the hind ones being slightly longer than the front; the feet should be small and oval, the tail long and tapering; the ears should be large in proportion, wide at the base, and pricked; the head long, with a good width between the eyes, narrowing in a straight line to a fine muzzle. The shape of the head however has varied over the years and has gradually become more pointed as breeders have concentrated on this aspect. The desire for the modern narrow, wedge head seems to me to be destroying one of the essential charms of the Siamese expression, that of wide-eyed innocence, cloaking the most mischievous intentions.

The eyes of the Siamese should be brilliant blue and oriental in shape, with no squint. At one time a kink in the tail and a squint were allowed, but these features are being bred out and are not liked in the Cat Show. The eyes of the Seal Point are commonly of darker blue than those of the Blue and Lilac Points, which are pure cerulean. The colouring of the Seal Point, with its dramatic contrast between dark brown and pale cream, has many admirers. But the subtle shades of the Chocolate, Lilac and Blue Points are very beautiful. The Blue Point should have points of a pale greyish-blue, of equal density. The body should be glacial white, shading gradually to blue-grey on the back. All types should have a short, fine coat, glossy and close-lying. Blue Points seem less aggressive than Seal Points; they are equally intelligent and attractive, but are perhaps gentler in character. Chocolate Points can be described as milk

Below, hide and seek round a basket. Note the large ears, long nose and beautiful oval paws of the well bred Siamese.

Opposite, who could resist the charm of this young kitten?

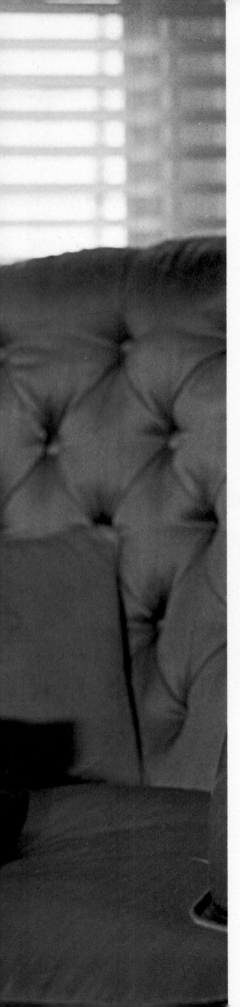

*An aristocratic and oriental
threesome belonging to the author.
Blue Magnolia, the television star,
Samson the Seal Point and Ming,
a brown Burmese kitten.*

*Above, Paul Hamlyn's beautiful
cat has all the characteristics of the
pedigree Siamese – the innocent
expression hides a marked ability
for stealing food.*

'My kittens may have valuable pedigrees and ought not to be left alone, but I can't ignore that bird any longer . . .'

Opposite, two cats who know how beautiful they are . . .

chocolate versions of the Seal Point; and Lilac Points* are a cross between Blue and Chocolate.

Siamese cats sometimes have an overloud vocal equipment; but not all Siamese are noisy and I myself am inclined to think that if a Siamese yells continuously – and some do – it is probably because it is bored. We have nearly always had in our home more than one Siamese at a time and none of them yelled. This may be mere coincidence, or we may just have been lucky. At mating times of course it is a different matter! Siamese are very gregarious and love company, either human or catty – or even doggy – for a Siamese readily pals up with other domestic animals.

But, whether noisy or not, Siamese all love to talk and one must be prepared to listen and reply. A Siamese will fix you with an azure stare and then start trying to

tell you some most important matter. It may be food, love, drama (another cat shut in the airing cupboard by mistake) or what have you; but the voice is importunate and you are compelled to listen. When a Siamese wants something it wants it NOW. And if you dare to take no notice it will find some other way of making you. In such circumstances one of our cats always bites our legs – gently of course.

Even the tiniest kitten has a will of iron. And woe betide you if you give in at the beginning. Your kitten may come to you at, say, two months, with a list of its requirements, including a diet sheet. But from the moment it arrives it will refuse to eat any of the recommended diet, like powdered milk, baby foods, pilchards, steamed fish and so on. Instead it will demand rabbit or chicken or some other delicacy and refuse all other food.

* Sometimes called 'Frost-Point' in America.

53

This is the moment you must be firm. The battle of wills is on. A Siamese is always prepared to go on hunger strike for days, secure in the belief – which must be handed down from mother to kitten – that you will give in first. But your kitten *must* be trained to eat a varied diet and so you *must* persevere; this is the vital test, which I myself have never yet won! All my cats eat what *they* like and never what I think they ought to eat.

But it is difficult to be dogmatic, if one can use that expression about cats' food. They are traditionally supposed to like fish and milk. None of ours have ever liked fish and only two have touched milk. Some of ours have thrived on dried meat and others on high protein processed foods, of which there are a number of brands on the market; some have eaten liver and some won't look at it; some have liked rabbit above all else, and others chicken. But none of ours will eat tinned cat meat and most of them have disliked raw meat. This is strange because a cat is a hunter and will go out and catch a mouse and presumably eat it. But if one of our cats ever caught a mouse I am sure they would bring it home in triumph to show off – and then form up for their usual dinner. I think Siamese are very individual about food and it is a matter of finding a diet which they like and which keeps them healthy. However, there are two very important additions to their daily diet which all cats must have; one is fresh water and the other is grass.

It is very important to try to teach your kitten to scratch on a log or scratching post from the very start. Once it gets a taste for furniture you are lost. A cat must scratch its claws, not only for sharpening

Blue Point stalking its prey; although they look rather exotic outside in green grass, Siamese are excellent hunters.

Right, not much room on the cat walk and the smallest comes off worst.

Above, Blue Magnolia – known as Maggie – is ready to resist all comers as she guards the bust of the author.

Tomkin, another of Sir John Smyth's cats, watching television with complete absorption.

purposes but to rub off the scale, which irritates; so it is up to you to train it to scratch in legitimate places. I know this can be done – though our cats just use the furniture! But at least they concentrate on some special bits, which is considerate of them.

There is quite an art in introducing a new kitten into an existing cat family and it can be dangerous for the new arrival if some precautions are not taken. One sometimes hears of two cats which have never made friends, and it may happen in spite of all your care. But I suspect that it is often because enough care was not taken in the first instance.

The method which we have suc-

cessfully adopted in the case of four different kittens is this. We purchased a wire play pen, with a lid, of sufficient size to take a blanket, litter tray, water bowl and food dish. Into this we put the new arrival in a room which we kept shut for the first few hours. When the kitten had settled down, with much petting and talking from us, and had been fed, we allowed the other cats, one at a time, to come into the room and smell the kitten through the wire. A certain amount of hissing takes place at this stage, but curiosity overcomes this after a little.

The introduction is repeated at intervals, with one of us always in the room, until a certain degree of

tolerance has been engendered. This may happen very quickly, or take a day or two. Meanwhile, from time to time, we let the kitten out to smell around and familiarize itself with its new surroundings. After a bit we let one of the other cats into the room too. If the older cat shows aggression we shut it out and try one of the others. We allow the cats to run free for short intervals, gradually getting to know each other, until we are satisfied that the kitten will not be attacked. After this the kitten is generally adopted quite happily by the others and there will be no further trouble. This method applies equally well to the introduction of a mature cat.

If you live in an apartment with no access to a garden it is still possible to keep a cat. All they need is a litter tray kept in a familiar place; but the tray must be cleaned every day as cats, particularly Siamese, are finicky over their daily habits. Siamese are often very modest and hate to be watched when using their tray. Cat litter is a little more expensive than peat, sawdust, earth or old newspapers, but a lot less trouble. It is entirely odourless and easy to clean with a small trowel or old spoon. So if the cat is not able to go out I do recommend the use of proper cat litter. The cats get quite used to living indoors and seem happy so long as they have company. But of course this applies only to neutered cats. Most vets think it best to neuter a cat quite early, before it has got a taste for sex! But it is best to take your own vet's advice on this matter.

There are of course many helpful organizations in the cat world. In England the Siamese Cat Club – whose efficient secretary, Mrs Mary Dunnill, is always most helpful with advice on any Siamese cat matters – runs a show every October. The President is that famous cat man, Sir Compton Mackenzie; and I have officiated for him at this show on several occasions. And there are many other smaller Siamese Cat Clubs, some of them specializing in the different colour points.

There is also a most helpful

organization called The Feline Advice Bureau, whose News Bulletin is packed with interesting advice on the health, feeding and boarding of cats – not only Siamese. They have a list of recommended catteries which is invaluable, as cat boarding establishments vary a good deal in efficiency.

London is well served with good vets, but there are also various organizations where free treatment and medical care can be obtained for those whose incomes do not allow for veterinary fees. There is the Blue Cross in Hugh St, Pimlico, whose premises are most efficient and up-to-date; and they also have hospitals at Grimsby and Hammersmith and a number of clinics. The People's Dispensary for Sick Animals have clinics distributed over the country; and they also have mobile vans which go into the small towns and villages, and a lovely Sanatorium at Ilford. The RSPCA, a name well known to all animal lovers, have welfare clinics all over the country and a new hospital in Holloway, North London.

I am kept up-to-date with Siamese cat interests in America by a most delightful man, Sam Scheer, who is the secretary of the Siamese Cat Society of America, Inc, which was founded way back in 1909, and now operates from 7335 South Elm Court, Littleton, Colorado 80120. And I have a cat fan in Wisconsin, whose letters have been a constant delight to me for many years. This girl, Janice Schade, suffered a severe illness when she was sixteen, the effects of which will be with her all her life and which prevent her from doing a normal job. But Jan has latterly found herself in the position of bread winner owing to the ill-health of her mother and step-father. Fortunately, some years ago, she had started a home-run business making cat toys and novelties, which she named Satra's Purr Palace after one of her Siamese pets. She herself is a devotee of the breed and has a number of these delightful animals whose behaviour she describes with great insight and humour. Her letters start off characteristically with 'Hi' and are followed by pages of anecdotes about her beloved Siamese and poodle dog.

From the other side of the world comes an interesting story which illustrates what a hold these tantalizing and enchanting creatures exert on their human owners. One day we had a letter from a Mrs Hamilton in Norfolk Island, 1,000 miles off the coast of Australia. She and her husband had two most beloved Siamese and were shocked to find, when they decided to move back to Australia, that the cats could not be admitted into the country without doing six months' quarantine in England, followed by a further sixty days in Australia – the cost of which would be about £300 or $750. When she wrote to me the cats had already been embarked at Sydney for transport to London. Mrs Hamilton knew no one in England; but in Norfolk Island she had read one of my cat books. She now implored me to visit her cats and let her know if they were all right. All she knew about the cattery to which her pets had gone was that it was in Chingford. After a certain amount of detective work we found the cattery and visited the two cats, who were in good health and well cared for. So we were able to write and send her some photos. Eventually the cats arrived safely back in Australia and were happily reunited, after a considerable journey and lapse of time; but the two Siamese had not forgotten their owners.

One of the most attractive qualities of the Siamese is this loyalty and devotion. A Siamese demands much more from you than food and warmth; it demands your love and attention. But once a proper relationship has been established your Siamese will remain devoted to you all its life, will show sympathy if you are ill, and concern if you are in trouble; and it will try to purr in your arms even when it is dying. Because a Siamese is such a personal cat there is, I think, a peculiar bond between Siamese cat owners all over the world and I hear regularly from addicts as far apart as Holland and South Africa, as well as from many parts of Great Britain: and when one hears of other people's Siamese one is made even more aware of how truly individual these cats are. Siamese have many attractions in common – their beauty, their charm, their gaiety, their intelligence, their mischievousness and their love; but the main thing they have in common is that they are uncommon. Uncommon cats they are and it is this star quality which makes them so constantly fascinating.

People often write to me on the interesting question of whether cats watch television. We had one Siamese, Tomkin, who always watched animal programmes, but most of ours have shown no interest in the box. One exception was Blue Magnolia, the subject of one of my books. The four cats we had at that time appeared in a film and a TV programme. When the photographic unit came to the apartment to take their photos the cameraman asked us to try to get the cats to do various things which he thought would make good television. Blue Magnolia was a most beautiful cat and she quite fancied herself in the role of film star. The other cats refused to have anything to do with this acting business, but Maggie performed her part perfectly. When the programme appeared we lined all four cats up to watch. Maggie sat entranced from the moment the programme started until the end. She then got down and walked off, graciously waving her tail, as if to say, 'Well folks, that's it.' But she never watched any other programme. It is hard not to imagine that she recognized herself. I think it is understandable that cats should watch moving animals, birds and so on; but strange that Maggie should have been interested only in that one programme.

But then Siamese are utterly unpredictable, and I would say to anyone who likes life to be full of unexpected dramas – get a Siamese cat!

Siamese are particularly graceful and will play for hours by themselves. They are equally good at playing with you, retrieving objects thrown for them or playing hide and seek.

Unusual breeds

CHRISTINE METCALF

There are hundreds and thousands of cats who belong to no particular breed, the ones who find their way into your home and heart. They are the result of years and years of free mating, the mongrel cats of this world, and may be found in many different colours and in many different situations. There are working cats, those kept on farms and in factories and warehouses to act as deterrents to rats and mice, and there are those who are just pets and conform to no particular standards because their owners want nothing more than to enjoy their company.

Many mongrel cats have as much care lavished on them as the most valuable pedigree cat, while others become the tough alley cats of the neighbourhood. People who are more discerning often visit a cat show so as to choose exactly the colour and type they have a fancy for. There are many cats from which to choose and it is as well to look around before making a decision, especially if something a little unusual is preferred. Whatever the final choice may be, the rewards are infinite for cats make ideal companions.

Most pedigree cats have been produced after a great deal of experimentation with colour and shape. When a breeder has a kitten with a feature he would like to perpetuate he very carefully prepares a breeding plan which he hopes will reproduce the chosen points. The whole process depends on genetics, the science of inheritance. Differences in development are due to the different genes. When the genes change they are known as 'mutations'. Often these mutations take unusual forms and cats different to the normal pattern are produced. This chapter will consider the unusual cats which are the result of these mutant genes.

All cats answer to one of two basic types, the British or Foreign type, but there is one exception – the Manx Cat. This is a friendly, rumbustious creature, very solid and British. The difference? The Manx Cat has no tail. There are several stories which give reasons for this lack of appendage. Some

Top left, a Long-haired Blue-Cream cat is a very beautiful Persian, but they are rather difficult to breed.

Top right, Manx cats have no tails and can be any colour; note the long hind legs.

Bottom left, a magnificent Abyssinian cat showing the unusual coat pattern.

Bottom right, a Long-haired Orange-eyed White cat – the orange eyes mean that the cat is not deaf like Blue-eyed cats.

Top, one blue eye and one orange eye for this white cat, and in America Odd-eyed whites are a recognized breed.

Left, a haughty looking Silver Tabby, and perhaps he has reason as they are particularly popular.

Bottom, Tortoishells rarely have the correct markings according to the show standards, but are always very beautiful.

people say that long ago the tails were cut off to decorate the shields of Irish warriors. To prevent this happening the anxious mother cats bit off the tails at birth. Another story says these cats are the descendants of the tailless Spanish cats which swam ashore after the Spanish Armada was repulsed. Noah is said to have cut off the cat's tail when he slammed the door of the Ark as the cat was the last to enter. These legends are fun but the reason is most likely to be a simple genetic inheritance. Tailless cats may be found in many parts of the world and there is no evidence to support the belief that they originated on the Isle of Man. However, in order that the breed shall not die, a cattery has been established on the island.

There is more to the Manx Cat than just being without a tail, and in a show specimen there should be a decided hollow at the end of the backbone while the rump should be as round as an orange. Manx Cats have a rabbity, or hopping gait, due to the hind legs being longer than the front. The head should be round and large, the nose longish, and the cheeks very prominent. The cheeks prevent the nose from appearing over elongated.

Americans say that snipeyness is a definite fault. The ears should be rather wide at the base, tapering off slightly to a point. The true Manx Cat, that is one with no tail whatsoever, is called a 'Rumpy', but there are Manx Cats of pure breeding that have a little bit of a tail, similar to a rabbit. These are called 'Stumpies'. When Rumpies are mated together consistently for several generations there is a high probability of producing a gene with a lethal factor which causes the kittens to die just before, or just after, birth. It makes the breeding of Manx Cats more difficult than other breeds and in the past it led to a decrease in the popularity of the breed, which fortunately is not the present situation. Manx Cats are now particularly popular again in the United States where it has been found that the best method of breeding, in order to eliminate the risk of the lethal factor, is to mate a good Rumpy to a Stumpy queen.

The coat of the Manx Cat is like that of a rabbit in that it is 'double', that is to say it has two layers, a top coat of soft open fur, with a thick soft undercoat. Manx Cats have a voice different to that of other cats, and when they are angry or excited they can make quite a lot of noise. They are intelligent and affectionate, gay and adaptable, and like dogs they will retrieve thrown objects. They are easy to train and will learn to walk well on a lead. They love having children around and to join in with their games.

Taillessness must be absolute in a show specimen. The coat and eye colour is immaterial. Recognized colours of Manx are the same as those recognized for Domestic Short-hairs, including parti-colour. The ideal eye colour should conform with the colour of the coat but it is only taken into account if all the other points are equal.

The first Abyssinian Cat was seen in England in 1869. It was said to have been imported from the country of its name but the evidence supporting this is rather vague since there are no cats of this type in Ethiopia today, except for those that have been taken there from Britain. The Abyssinian Cat is a Foreign type Short-hair, long and svelte. It is said to resemble closely the cats worshipped long ago in Ancient Egypt, and is very like the Caffre Cat from which it is said the early domestic cats were descended.

Normally the colour and pattern of a cat's coat is made up by the intermingling of hairs of different

colours. The Abyssinian Cat, however, has an unusual colour pattern because each hair has two or three separate bands of colour on it. The ground colour is a lovely shade of russet brown, with each hair being banded with black or dark brown. This colouring is similar to that of a wild rabbit and for this reason Abyssinians are sometimes called 'Rabbit' or 'Bunny' cats.

Although the Abyssinian resembles the Siamese in many ways it should not be too extreme in outline. The body should be medium long, lithe and graceful, but showing well-developed muscular strength. The tail should be thick at the base, fairly long and tapering, tipped with black; the ears should not be as large as those of the Siamese. The eyes should be green, yellow or hazel, and should be large, bright and expressive. Abyssinians often show tabby markings and bars on the head, legs and tail. Breeders of champions seek to breed out these marks as it is a fault and no heavily barred entrant would be awarded a championship. A good specimen

showing a dark line running up the spine, however, would not be penalized. Another common fault in this breed, and one that is difficult to breed out, is a touch of white about the chin and throat. Ideally the chin should be cream; the inside of the forelegs and belly should be orange brown. The pads of the feet should be black with this colour extending up the back of the hind legs.

Red Abyssinians are a different colour and now have a breed class all their own. Abyssinians tend to have small litters, seldom more than four, and more of them are males than females. They are, like Siamese, 'one-man' cats. They have plenty of character and like the Manx they talk a lot. Abyssinians can be trained to the collar and lead and will retrieve objects thrown to them. They love travelling in cars and trains when it means they need not be separated from their owners.

Mutant genes can cause unusual features apart from creating new breeds. One very common mutation often causes a condition known as

Butter wouldn't melt in the mouth of this brown Abyssinian . . . but the Long-haired, blue-eyed Persian lets you know straight away when he wants something.

Left, not all Blue-Cream cats are Persians, this is a Short-haired cat with the same delicate colouring.

Right, an American Maine Coon cat.

Bottom right, a cat found only in America is the Peke-faced Persian.

'polydactilism', which is when a domestic cat possesses extra toes. A normal cat has five toes on each forefoot and four on each hindfoot. The extra digits may occur on front or back feet and there are variations as to number. Polydactilism is known to be inherited but details of the inheritance are unknown. Geneticists have concluded that the extra toes are a characteristic of a dominant gene and because of this it is passed on from generation to generation. A kitten not itself showing this malformation can transmit extra toes to subsequent generations when it has a history of polydactilism among its forebears. Theodore Roosevelt's pet, 'Slippers', was a cat with six toes on each foot.

Another curious condition is the deafness which often goes with blue eyes when the colour of the coat is white. White cats have a tendency to deafness and it has been the aim of breeders to eliminate this fault. There is no doubt that the trait is hereditary and even after several generations it can recur. A peculiar aspect of the condition is that some

Blue-eyed, White-haired kittens have been known to be deaf until they are a few months old. The blue eye colour has changed as the kitten grows and the cat has then been able to hear.

There is no real explanation for this but a geneticist working in the 1920s believed that when the eye colour was sufficiently intense to invade the inner eyes it might also invade the inner ear. He had noticed a similar abnormality in white dogs with blue eyes.

In spite of these breeding problems the Blue-eyed White Long-hairs are a very desirable breed although still one of the rarest in Britain. It is probably one of the oldest breeds and is descended from the Angora and Persian. The Angora had a less woolly coat than the Persian; it was much lighter boned, the nose was longer and it had up-right ears. White in cats is a dominant colour, therefore a white cat must always have at least one white parent: it can never be a throwback. White cats are not albino cats, and this condition is very rare. If you

mate an albino cat with a coloured cat the gene for colour development becomes re-activated and the kittens will show the concealed colour of the albino parent. The eyes of an albino cat are not the same as those of a normal cat; they are pink and the vision is poor in daylight.

There are five varieties of white cats; two Long-haired, two British Short-hairs and the White Manx. As a result of trying to improve the standard of the Blue-eyed Whites other cats were introduced into the mating pattern. It has been suggested that some breeders introduced an Orange-eyed Black Persian. Whatever the cause the vivid orange eyes were transferred to the white coat and as recently as 1960 the Orange-eyed White was given a breed registration by the Governing Council of the Cat Fancy in Britain.

For a long time Orange-eyed Whites have been more numerous than Blue-eyed Whites, probably because their comparative freedom from the handicap of deafness has meant that breeders tend to use them

as a mate for a Blue-eyed queen. Many of the British Orange-eyed Whites fail badly in eye colour; it is difficult to obtain a really vivid orange but breeders are overcoming this difficulty and now some of the best specimens are to be found in Britain.

The Blue-eyed White Short-hair has the same handicap of deafness as the Long-hair, and it is most odd that when a British White is born with a black mark on the forehead, or some black hairs in the coat (it can vary from a black smudge like a fingerprint to just a few hairs) this seems to guarantee good hearing and is looked upon as a good sign by

the breeder because the dark colour will fade but the hearing will not be impaired. White cats born with green eyes are not recognized as a breed by the associations in either Britain or America, and although they make very attractive pets they cannot take part in competition.

Eyes are important in the next unusual breed of cats. The Odd-eyed White is not an accepted breed in Britain but in America it has a breed class and number. In an attempt to breed out the tendency to deafness, Blue-eyed Whites have been cross mated with Orange-eyed Whites, the result occasionally producing these unusual kittens, with

one orange eye and one blue eye.

Some owners of white cats with odd eyes believe that the cat has deficient hearing on the side of the blue eye, but there is no evidence to support this. The American Cat Fanciers' Association accept the Odd-eyed White for competition in the classes for Persian, Manx, Rex and Domestic Short-hairs. The colour must be pure, clear white with no coloured hairs. One eye must be' deep blue and the other vivid orange. There are objections to dark hairs, a cream or bluish tinge in the coat, and to pale eye colour.

Most white cats take a pride in their appearance; they are very

Top left, one of the rare Long-haired Tortoiseshell cats.

Bottom left, a Long-haired cream Persian.

Right, an elegant Short-haired Tortoiseshell cat.

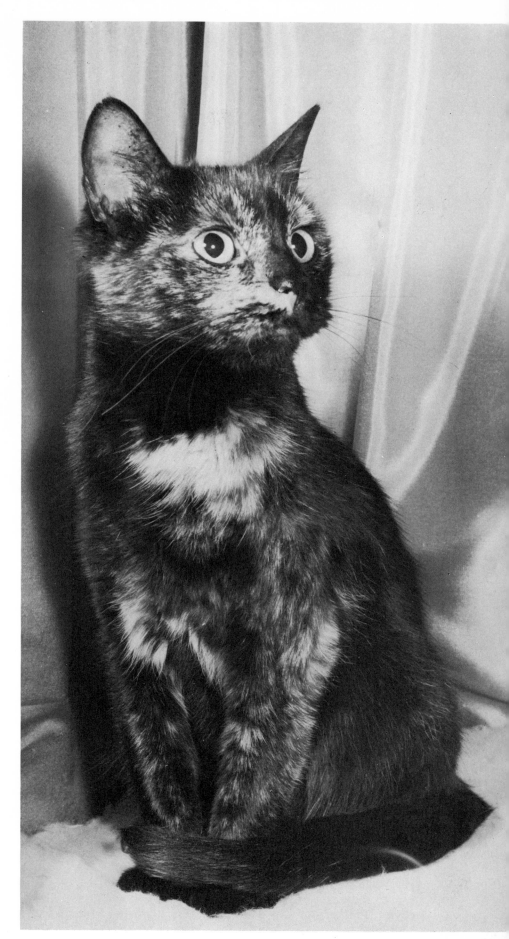

fussy and spend a great deal of time washing and grooming themselves. The female cats are usually very much smaller than the male, and with their beautiful eyes and lovely white coats they have a decidedly feminine look. They need only a little help from their owner to maintain a good appearance. A daily grooming to remove old hairs should be the practice for all cats; other than this all that is required to remove mud and grease marks, especially round the tail where there is a tendency to yellowing, is a sprinkling with talcum powder or a suitable dry shampoo and a quick brush.

It is important to keep all long-haired cats well groomed. The long coat calls for constant attention, and will otherwise become felted and tangled. Loose hair must be removed or it will be swallowed by the cat during washing. To look really magnificent for a show the long coat may be polished with a piece of silk or chamois leather.

A breed of cats recognized only in the United States is the Peke-faced Persian. This breed has developed because some of the Red and Red Tabby Long-hairs produced offspring with heavy jowls like a Pekinese dog and it is from its appearance that the name is derived. They should conform to the standards set forth for the Solid Red and Red Tabby colours; any other colour is a disqualification. The head of this cat resembles that of a Pekinese dog, and not only must the forehead be high but it must also bulge over the nose to create a sharp stop. The nose should be very short, depressed and indented between the eyes. In profile the nose should be

so short as to be hidden by the full, round cheeks. The muzzle should be decidedly wrinkled with folds of skin from each side of the nose and under the eye sockets. The American standards describe it as having a cascading of skin from under the eyes. A regrettable aspect of this extra skin is the fact that the tear ducts tend to become blocked so that the eyes are apt to water a great deal. The tears streaming continually down the cat's face stain the fur and spoil the animal's appearance.

Like the Pekinese dog, the cat's eyes are prominent and have a different expression to that of other Persian cats. Frequently the Pekinese dog suffers from irregularities of the teeth and underjaw. When these deformities occur in the cat they are considered to be a fault, as also are ears that are upright and set close together. In every other

way this cat conforms to the standards set forth for Persians. The coat should be long and fine in texture, soft, glossy and full of life. It should be long all over the body, including the shoulders. The ruff should be immense and continue in a deep frill between the front legs. The ear furnishing should be long and curved and the tail plume should be very full.

The United States has another breed of cats which is all its own. The Maine Coon Cat has no official show standing but it is a domestic variant. New Englanders once thought that it was a cross between a cat and a racoon, but the idea is quite inconceivable. The cat received its name from the fact that its legs show a slight toeing in effect similar to a racoon, and from its coat which is said to resemble the animal. The head is pointed and the eyes, though perfectly round, often show

A Long-haired Tortoishell and White or 'Calico' cat as they are called in America.

Right, a beautifully striped tabby puts up a helping paw to get the last drop of malt.

Above, this little silver tabby kitten's delicate black markings make him one of the most striking of all the breeds.

Left, a Long-haired brown tabby.

a slight slant. Although the Maine Coon Cat is believed to be descended from the long-haired tabbies that went wild when the early settlers took them to America, the tail is the reverse of that of the Persian, having the longest hairs at the base instead of at the tip. The fur is thick and longish and can be many colours. There have been Coon Cats in Maine for more than a hundred years.

The Mexican Hairless has almost disappeared from the American scene, and is thought to be nearly extinct. It is not a very beautiful cat and probably this is the reason for its rejection. The name of this cat is somewhat misleading, as it does in fact have some very short, close hair. The Mexican Hairless began as a mutation which was then culti-

vated, but its appearance was so unprepossessing, looking something like a cross betwen a cat and a rat, that it did not gain many admirers – and it is popular demand that makes a breeder persevere with a new variety. This cat has large ears and a bare tail like a rat, the neck and underparts are pinkish and the back is mouse-coloured. It is adapted to extremes of temperature and in winter develops a ridge of fur along the back and upper surface of its tail. The elegant Persians would look with disdain upon this ugly duckling if ever it made an entrance at a show.

In complete contrast breeders are becoming increasingly interested in Long-haired Blue-Cream cats. Invariably these cats are female, and are the result of cross breeding between Blue Persians and Cream Persians. The Governing Council of the Cat Fancy in Britain says that the shades of blue and cream should be softly intermingled pastel shades. Any patches of colour are frowned upon and it isn't easy to achieve a cat without some cream patches or a paw in solid colour. However, a cream patch on the head (a blaze) is acceptable, and in America the Blue-Creams may be patched as well as intermingled.

Geneticists have worked out a definite formula for breeding from Blues and Creams, so that the offspring are predictable in colouration. This colour inheritance is one of the rare examples of sex linkage in animals. When a Cream male is mated to a Blue female the male kittens will be Blue, the females Blue-Cream. A Blue male crossed with a Cream female will similarly produce Blue-Cream female kittens and the males will be Cream. When a Blue-Cream female is mated to a Blue male she could have Blue males, Cream males, Blue females or Blue-Cream females. When the father is Cream the colour pattern is reversed, giving rise to Blue males, Cream males, Cream females and Blue-Cream females. For someone interested in breeding both colours a Blue-Cream Long-hair is an excellent beginning. Blue-Creams have also been known occasionally to appear among the litters of Tortoiseshells.

It is curious how this factor for

sex predisposition crops up in the Tortoiseshell and in breeds allied to it. The number of Long-haired Tortoiseshells is small as these cats are almost always female. When a male does appear it is invariably sterile. This factor even appears in the Tortie Point Siamese, although in this cat only the points are Tortoiseshell. Few Tortoiseshells conform closely to the standards laid down with their patching of red, cream, and black. Each area of colour should be distinct from the other, with the cream and red being as bright as possible. It is difficult to obtain a red that is rich enough, or one that carries the required patching in equal quantities. The patches occur all over, including the paws and the ears. Any tabby markings, stripes or bars, or any solid colour on the face, legs or tail, would lose points in competition. Many breeders like to see a blaze of red or cream on the face, running down from the forehead, but this is not a requirement of the standard. When mating the queen with a stud of one of the body colours, it is not possible to forecast the colour of the kittens, as it is with the Blue-Cream.

Closely connected to the Tortoise-shell Long-hair, and one that cannot be bred to order, is the Tortoise-shell and White Long-hair. New Englanders call their breed the 'Calico Cat'. The American Cat Fanciers' Association require the white markings to be limited to certain areas so that the cat appears to have been dropped into a can of paint. This is another breed in which males are extremely rare. Anyone interested in learning about cat breeding would need to follow a complicated breeding chart in order to get the right genetic pattern. Many breeders have been experimenting for years with various matings and have yet been unsuccessful in obtaining the desired amount of red, cream and black patches, interspersed with not too much white.

The pattern of Tabby Cats is either striped or blotched, and both patterns never appear together on one cat. Mate a cat with a blotched pattern to a cat with a striped pattern and the resulting kittens will be striped because the gene for striped patterning is dominant. The classic pattern for the Tabby Cat

should be as distinct as possible, and it is not easy to breed a cat whose markings conform exactly to the standards required. Even though breeders have difficulty in breeding out tabby markings on other breeds of cats, the bars and stripes rarely conform to the pattern. On a good specimen of Tabby Cat the stripes and bars across the shoulders should, when viewed from the top, resemble butterfly wings.

The Blotched Tabby has longitudinal stripes forming a horseshoe or circular pattern. There must be at least one clear circle running round the throat and chest, and these are referred to as 'mayoral chains' or 'necklaces'. The legs and tail must be marked evenly with rings. The cheeks should have two definite swirls running from the corners of the eyes, and there should be delicate pencillings on the head and face in a clear black. On the forehead these marks often form a letter 'M'. Is this the initial for Mahommet? Legend tells us that the mark on the shoulders is the imprint left by the hand of Mahommet when he caressed the cat.

Long-haired Tabbies and Short-

haired Tabbies may be Brown, Red, or Silver in Britain, but in the United States there is an additional colour, the Blue Tabby, which has any icy-blue white ground colour with dense darker blue markings in the Persian. The ground colour of the Domestic Short-hair should be pale blue with tan overtones, and again the markings should be a dense dark blue. Shakespeare was writing of a tabby when he referred to a 'Brindled' cat.

Less often seen at shows now but gradually making a come-back is the Mackerel Tabby, which is marked differently to the usual Tabby, having fine vertical stripes, like a mackerel, instead of the conventional target pattern. The rings must be as narrow and numerous as possible, running from the spine towards the ground.

There is a rare Siamese type of cat that is solid grey in colour with amber-green eyes, and it actually comes from Thailand where it is equally rare. A male and a female were eventually taken to the United States and now Korats are beginning to make their appearance at the cat shows, having demonstrated that

they can be bred successfully. These cats are of the Foreign type, and several generations of breeding true must pass before they can become an accepted breed.

In the United States Domestic Short-hairs have the same colours and patterns as the British cats but they differ in that the size of the head is slightly smaller and less broad. Other cats found in the United States are very similar to the British cats but their heads are rounder and the ears are even smaller; these are the exotic cats, the jungle cats which have been domesticated.

Mostly such animals are bought from pet shops because they are nearly always jungle born; only a few are bred by cat fanciers. The most common are the Ocelot and the Margay. Although it is illegal in some cities to keep a wild animal, a case can be made out for keeping either of these wild cats because they develop into such delightful pets and can very easily be domesticated. There are, of course, differences to which the owners must adjust. For example, they are nocturnal creatures so that bedtime can become a little hectic. Their claws and

Far left, a magnificent spotted cat looking very like its larger cousin the leopard. They are difficult to breed for show purposes as the judges don't like stripy tails.

Above left, a Korat cat from Thailand which was bred in America.

Above right, ocelots make exotic and charming pets.

teeth are more to be reckoned with than those of the domestic cat, but once these problems are overcome they make unusual and very affectionate pets.

An ocelot looks rather like a small leopard. The ground colour of the coat is light, warm beige, and overall there are black rings and spots; the tail is almost half the length of the body. Margays are very similar in appearance to the Ocelot, and in fact it is difficult to distinguish between the kittens of the two. But Margays are not as large when fully grown, being about the size of the Domestic cat, whereas an Ocelot can weigh up to 60 pounds. Both animals really are exotic, and as pets they are quite impressive.

The cat as aesthete

BEVERLEY NICHOLS

A cat appears in Chapter One of my first novel, a school story which was published – I have to confess it – over forty years ago. It is a black kitten to whom I gave the name of Pasht, and it lies purring on the bed of my young hero, on his last night at home before he sets out to face the rigours of Marlborough College, which in those days was very rigorous indeed. All round his room are hung pictures of cats; there is a china cat on the mantelpiece – I still have it. And, rather to my surprise, there is a reference to Baudelaire. I had forgotten that Baudelaire was a cat lover.

So I may with some justice claim that cats have played a considerable part in my life for quite a considerable time. As it was in the beginning, so it is today. There is still a cat purring on my bed upstairs, a large tabby called Leo, with a quite exceptional propensity for mischief. Shortly, no doubt, he will descend to make his tour of inspection, jump on my desk, and play havoc with this manuscript. As I look out of the window I see another cat, a very sedate and decorous ginger called Hugo, walking across the lawn towards the lily-pond. This might seem to bode ill for the goldfish, but as it happens, he never catches anything. As the morning goes by other cats will probably put in an appearance – not mine, but callers from neighbouring houses, who are always welcome.

Some people might think that everything worth writing about cats had already been written. This, of course, would be a very foolish assumption, for every cat is a multi-coloured personality, worthy of endless study and consideration. And needless to say, every owner of every cat – if one can ever be described as 'owning' so individual and independent a creature – will find various aspects of the feline personality which specially interest him. So it is with myself. For me, not unnaturally, my most constant interest is centred on the connection that cats may – or may not have – with the arts. My profession is the art of letters; my greatest love is the art of music; and I have always had a

Beverley Nichols feeding some stray dock cats in Sydney.

Right, cats and kittens love looking at themselves in mirrors as they are fully aware of how beautiful they are.

passionate concern for the visual arts. When I make a garden I do not work as a botanist but as a designer, experimenting in line and colour and what the Impressionists used to call 'significant form'. And when I have finished, when the picture, as it were, is complete, I am inclined to lose interest. This is an unfortunate and extremely expensive personal characteristic, because it means – has constantly meant – that one must uproot oneself, sell the house, buy another one, and start all over again.

Cats and art, cats and music, cats and gardens and flowers . . . is there anywhere a connecting link? Are we carrying anthropomorphism to extremes if we suggest that cats, being

the most beautiful, graceful and responsive of God's creatures, are thereby endowed with an aesthetic sense?

I think not.

Let us come from the general to the particular.

I first began to have an inkling of this 'aesthetic sense' some twenty years ago, when studying the behaviour patterns of my first Siamese cat whose name was 'One'. This was a very fitting appelation, for he was top of all the feline classes, in brains, in beauty, and in bravery.

One had eyes of the most piercing blue, and his favourite sleeping place was a cushion of sapphire blue silk. For some time I assumed that this was a mere coincidence, albeit a very

'If people are going to write about me, I want to read what they say and there is something here which I think could be altered slightly . . .'

Top right, one might think that a tabby would have a problem in choosing a background to set off his colouring, but this cat seems to have found the answer.

Bottom left, 'the supreme aesthete' Santa, the Tortoishell cat in her own particular armchair.

Bottom right, cats will sometimes accept you as a partner in the game, but more often they prefer to perform their own dances among the leaves.

Left, Hugo, the author's ginger cat, demonstrates his sense of colour as he poses against the azaleas.

Below, two of the author's cats, Hugo and Leo, waiting for an audience before beginning one of their 'ballets'.

happy one. But then, as summer came, and as I took to following him round the garden, I began to wonder. Why was it that he invariably chose to lie down in the shadow of a clump of lupins, whose colour so perfectly matched his own? Why, when the lupins were finished, did he dispose himself beside the delphiniums? As the year went by it was blue, always blue. And when Spring came round again, he headed straight for the scillas and the grape hyacinths, and ended up by sleeping in a copse among the bluebells.

You may say that this was a matter of pure chance, or even a sort of protective camouflage instinct, inherited from a distant past, springing from the same complex of physical and psychical reflexes that painted the stripes on the coat of the tiger. This seems a prosaic explanation, though there may be some truth in it. I still prefer my own interpretation –

that cats have an aesthetic sense.

Consider the portrait of my own tortoiseshell cat Santa, who blends so subtly with the daring design of the armchair which was her favourite point of vantage. There was never any reason why Santa should wish to camouflage herself; no dangers threatened her, no harsh words were ever spoken. And yet, from the moment when she first arrived, as an extremely alluring kitten, she went straight for this armchair, gazed at it, sniffed it, jumped up into it, curled round, and adopted it as her permanent and exclusive property.

Is it so foolish to assume that in Santa's mind some strange, mystical, aesthetic appreciation was at work? You think so? Then why does my ginger cat so often choose to repose himself under the copper beech, where he makes a picture of such enchanting harmonies, and why does he invariably avoid any background

Kittens are just as good as cats when it comes to balancing tricks.

with a suggestion of pink? Bronze and red and orange, but never pink? If you deposit him in a bed of pink phlox he is outraged, and he will not be seen in the neighbourhood of pink roses. Camouflage? No, because he lies most contentedly on the open lawn, and his favourite chair, in the summer, has a covering of white linen.

The subtlest answer to this question is also the simplest. Hugo, at heart, is an artist. He realizes that he is beautiful. (All cats have a charming tendency to admire themselves in mirrors.) And when Hugo is choosing his backgrounds, he chooses them for the excellent reason that he knows which settings will show him to the greatest advantage.

Again, from the general to the particular.

Of all the arts to which cats are attracted, none seems to make a greater appeal than the art of ballet. True, some other animals dance, in a clumsy sort of way. Dolphins plunge about with an endearing exuberance, penguins slither down their icy slopes, like children romping on Hampstead Heath. And then there is that exotic bird, whose name I always forget, which so constantly appears on television, strutting up and down before its mate in a stately sexual ritual. But none of these, or any other creatures that I know of, really *dance*, for the sheer aesthetic joy of it. And surely, it is highly significant that one of the most generally accepted of all the classical movements in the ballet has been given, inevitably, the name of *entrechat*.

All of my cats have been accomplished dancers, and I like to think that the reason why they have usually reached a rather exceptional peak of accomplishment is because their master has appreciated their

Practising for going on the stage?

82

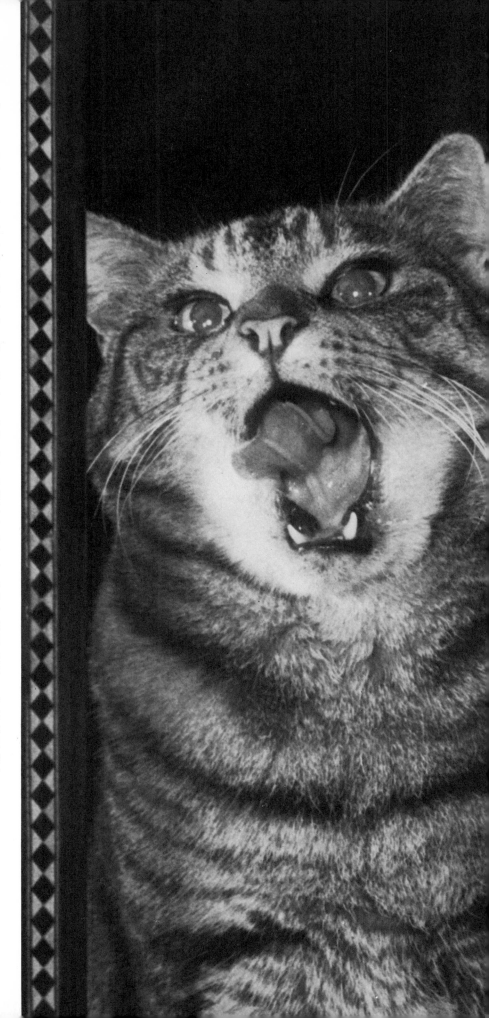

potentialities, and done his best to develop them. Thus, in my present garden, there are three main 'stages' on which feline ballets are currently performed, and two of them were specially designed by myself for dancing purposes.

The first of these 'stages' is a large sloping bank, thickly planted with various types of heather. Admittedly, I did not design this feature *solely* for purposes of the ballet; heathers are beautiful and rewarding in their own right. But from the moment that the first of them was planted, I realised their ballet potentialities. I therefore arranged drifts of the white *Erica carnea*, which flowers in mid-winter when ballet stages are not easily available. I also contrived a considerable expanse of heathers with russet foliage, to enhance the talents of a highly accomplished ginger cat, and of golden heathers as a background for a black cat, who was not only a dancer, but a choreographer of considerable ingenuity.

Once the stages were set, and the heathers fully grown, nothing remained but to deposit the cats among them, and wait for the ballets to begin. And begin they did, from the word one, without a hint of prompting from myself. In and out of the heathers they whirled, performing the most astonishing *entrechats*, in a series of exquisite and complicated rhythmic designs, using even their tails to emphasize their art. One was reminded of Fonteyn and Nureyev. (If nature had endowed Nureyev with a tail, one hardly dare contemplate the heights to which he might have risen.)

The other two ballets which are permanently in the repertoire go by the names of '*Fenilles d'Automne*' and '*L'Escalier*'. The first explains itself, being a series of complicated variations composed around the falling leaves of the copper beech. This is the ballet with which we invariably open the autumn season, and its popularity shows no sign of waning. The second ballet, '*L'Escalier*', is quite different, completely modern, and calling for such a high standard of technique that not all cats are able to give perfect performances in it, though all are willing to try. It is danced round a pair of steps which I

place in the centre of the lawn on summer evenings. As soon as the steps are in position, the cats emerge from the wings – which are situated in the shrubbery – stalk slowly across the lawn, like ballerinas preparing for a new variation in Swan Lake, sniff the steps, pat them, walk up them, and down again, and then the dance begins. It is a long ballet, far too intricate to describe on paper, but it holds the attention of the audience from the first moment to the last. And when I say 'audience' I mean precisely that; for cats do quite definitely demand an audience of at least one human being. If the audience is unappreciative, or restive, or in any way neglectful, the ballet comes to an abrupt full-stop; the cats retire with offended dignity

to the wings, and can only with difficulty be persuaded to resume their positions.

This feline propensity for ballet leads us inevitably to a consideration of the feline attitude to music. Here we enter very difficult psychological territory, hitherto – as far as I am aware – uncharted. With dogs, of course, it would be a simple matter. Dogs are totally unmusical. True, I once met a dog whom I credited for a short time with a musical sense. This was a charming black retriever who, as soon as anybody turned on a record of the Beatles, emitted a howl of the most piercing intensity. 'This,' I thought, 'shows great musical intelligence. The poor creature is evidently in acute distress, as indeed am I.' But a few minutes later the

Intricate ballet movements performed with poise and elegance.

record was changed to one of Menuhin playing Elgar's Violin Concerto, and the howls of the dog became louder and more agonized.

With cats it is very different. The immediate reaction of a kitten, hearing the piano for the first time, is one of sheer terror. Even if one plays with the soft pedal depressed, and strikes a few muted chords, pianissimo, in the treble, the kitten takes swift refuge under the sofa. But this stage does not last for long; curiosity impels the kitten to emerge from its retreat, and eventually to jump up onto the piano in order to peer inside the instrument, and take furtive dabs at the hammers as they strike the wires. This, of course is a purely mechanical reaction.

What is going on in the kitten's *brain?* And later on, in the cat's? What is the music saying to them? If it comes to that, is it saying anything at all?

I am reasonably certain that it is, and I have a good deal of evidence for this conviction. My most striking witness is a cat called 'Five'. (There was a time when all my cats were known by numbers.) Five, who died in my arms, still faintly purring, at the age of 21, was a very impressive personality. On the days when the garden was open to the public he used to station himself in my servant's sitting-room, placing himself in the centre of the table, in order to receive homage from the visitors. They paid sixpence each for the privilege of stroking him, and many charitable causes were

thereby considerably enriched.

But we were speaking of music, and in this connection Five gave the most effective demonstration of musical taste that one could demand. For Five loved – really did love – nightingales. Not as birds, but as songsters. When I first discovered him, one magical night in June, sitting under the pear tree, gazing up at the small feathered creature who was sending her fountains of liquid melody to the stars, I naturally – being human – drew the worst conclusions. I said to myself 'Five is waiting to pounce on the nightingale, and that would be too much to bear.' Harsh words were spoken, reproachful glances were exchanged, and Five stalked away, while the nightingale sang on.

But he was soon back again. As I sat there in the shadows I began to realize that it was not the bird that fascinated him, but the music. The bird fluttered quite close to him, on a lower branch, but he did not stir. Nor did he make the least attempt to conceal himself; he stayed on the moonlit grass, in full view of the bird. And when the song was over he walked slowly back to the house, like an elederly opera-lover going home after a particularly moving performance of *La Bohème*.

You may dismiss this as a fairy-tale. It happens to be a strictly factual account of an incident in my life which I shall not easily forget, and which I believe to have correctly interpreted. For if Five was not listening to the music, what was he listening to? What was going on in the feline brain?

The feline brain! Aye, 'there's the rub', one might say, pausing to stroke an obliging tabby. It is an astonishing brain, of exquisite subtlety, and very few men take the trouble to interpret it. I have often

This cat has the air of a dedicated musician.

felt that cats have a psychic quality, and obviously I am not alone in this opinion. Why, otherwise, should cats have been associated throughout history with witchcraft and every form of necromancy? Why were they deified in Egypt and execrated in the Middle Ages? Why, in every country and in every stage of civilization is the black cat an emblem of good fortune?

And why – perhaps the most significant question of all – is there this universal legend that 'cats can see in the dark'? From the purely optical point of view there is no foundation whatever for such a belief. A cat in the dark, as far as material objects are concerned, is as sightless as any other animal. But there is no doubt whatever that cats often do see something, not only in the dark but by daylight, which is invisible to the rest of the animal kingdom. Sit with a cat at the window of a basement room, with no outside prospect but a blank wall – no flowers, no trees, no birds, no shadow. Watch its eyes as they stare at this apparent nothingness. Note the swift movements of the ears, the inexplicable twitchings of the tail. These physical reflexes are not merely manifestations of a sort of nervous twitch, they are the direct response to some outside stimulus, which, to ourselves, is invisible, inaudible, and altogether non-existent. Surely, once again, we are confronted with a phenomenon of which the simplest explanation is also the most likely to be true? Cats have indeed a psychic sense.

Maybe it is this psychic element which makes them objects of such terror to so many otherwise normal and well-balanced men and women, though not every scientist would agree with this interpretation. Recently, in America, experiments were made in this connection with a hundred babies, of all shapes and sizes, gathered together in a hospital ward. Eight per cent of the babies, when placed in the vicinity of a cat, showed signs of great distress, even though they could not see it or hear it. The scientists came to the conclusion that the babies' distress must therefore be associated with the sense of smell, giving evidence of some allergy in the olfactory organs.

I do not believe this, for the very excellent reason that several good friends of mine, who love and deeply admire the feline race, are violently affected by asthma if they even sit in a chair where a cat has been lying. A love or a hatred of cats has nothing to do with the olfactory organs. We have to search a great deal deeper for the true explanation.

But it is with the cat as an aesthete that we were primarily concerned, and if some readers may feel that these arguments have been conducted on too remote and highfalutin a level, I would remind them that even in the most humdrum and prosaic activities of life cats display a refinement which is not to be matched in the behaviour of any other animal. Consider a very obvious example – the toilet procedure. When cats wish to do this they seem to realize, even from the time when they are very small kittens, that it is a matter which, if it is to be inoffensive, must be conducted with delicacy and dispatch. It is as though some Feline Sanitary Inspector, countless thousands of years ago, had drawn up a code of rules for the proper routine, which cats have instinctively followed ever since. The selection of the earth, the discreet adoption of the correct pose, and when the operation is finished, the swift, sure strokes of the front paws so that all traces are completely concealed . . . this ritual may not come under the heading of aesthetics, but it certainly ranks high in the realm of etiquette, and maybe the two are not so far apart.

The sun is high, I write on a golden morning of Spring, and as I look out of the window I see my small companions, most obligingly, putting my theories into practice. Hugo sits among the daffodils – deep auburn against the palest yellow. Leo lies in the dappled shadow of the old apple tree, listening to the carolling of a thrush, with evident pleasure. They exchange glances, tails began to twitch, there is music in the breeze, maybe they are thinking of a new ballet. But it will not begin until I go out to watch, so I must lay down the pen. Cats, as I earlier reminded you, demand an audience. As long as I am around, they will always have one.

Can cats see in the dark? Do they have some psychic quality? Certainly one would never know what this large-eyed tabby was thinking.

American and British show cats

MAY EUSTACE

Today, after one hundred years of pedigree cats, there has come into the cat lover's vision a new state, a new establishment, a new domain, known as the world of show cats. It has been nurtured and developed from experiences and experiments of cat breeders during many decades. With knowledge and understanding of the nature of cats, and with sympathy and understanding between enlightened cat lovers, this new precinct has been created.

The culmination of a cat fancier's ambition is to own and exhibit a show cat. This special variety was unknown one hundred years ago. Horse racing, dog racing, cock fighting, competitions and exhibitions were found to be interesting and were an outlet for man's quest for adventure. With the dawn of the nineteenth century a new awareness of things, people and creatures was created and with this new awareness a spirt of adventure came and set up new values and new ways of thinking. Shows came into existence, and introduced a stimulant not hitherto envisaged.

In 1859 the first dog show was recorded, but it was not until 1871 that the first cat show took place at the Crystal Palace in London. This was something entirely different. Cat fever seized a certain section of the community, and wonder and astonishment at the mere thought of a cat show manifested itself among sober-minded citizens. The names associated with the first ventures were all male, among them Harrison Weir, J. Jenner Weir, John Jennings, W. J. Nichols, P. H. Jones, Dr Gordon Staples and J. Millett. Later on women entered the cat's world both as writers, exhibitors and judges. The greatest woman fancier of a slightly later age was Frances Simpson, whose publication *The Book of the Cat* is still the bible on which many fanciers pin their faith.

Not all fanciers approved of male domination over the cat world, and in America Helen M. Winslow, writing in 1900, expressed concern. She wrote of the judging establishment in America:

'American cat shows have at least three judges, and one at least

A champion Long-haired White and his jubilant owner.

90

should be a woman. A cat should be handled gently and kept as calm as possible during the judging. Women are naturally more gentle in their methods, and more tender-hearted. When my pets are entered for competition may some wise, kind woman have the judging of them.'

It is a nice thought that such kind words about women fanciers should be written up for posterity by an American.

Once cat shows were established on the right lines, and a system of points judging had been agreed and found satisfactory, cat shows became socially acceptable to the cat lovers of the world. Interest generated by the first London show created developments in other parts of England and Scotland. The Metropolitan Show held in 1875 at the Gymnasium in Edinburgh had an entry of 560 cats, the largest ever recorded up till then. According to judges' reports their quality had not hitherto been exceeded. H. G. Brown was the originator and J. Billett the organizer. Exhibitors were appreciative of these first endeavours and gifts given to organizers included a silver tankard to Harrison Weir and a gold medal to J. Billett.

The naming of classes for exhibition is interesting to fanciers today: He Cats, She Cats, Geldings, Large Cats and Small Cats were shown in classes for Firemen, Cabmen, Cottagers, Pensioners, and Lords and Ladies. But it was the Ladies, just new to the Fancy, who added the greatest glamour to the first show cats. Many of the first cat clubs were almost entirely peopled by the British aristocracy. In America too we found affinity with some of the most notable in the land. Quickly following the first British show, the first American cat show was recorded in Madison Square Garden, New York, in 1895, for which the pioneer show manager, James H. Hyde, had brought from England the schedules of the Crystal Palace shows. Soon the cult for cat shows spread to many states. British-bred cats were foremost in the winning classes. As in Britain, and other parts of the world, the show cat, once recognized and loved,

had really and truly come to stay.

Interest gathered momentum, and the breeding of pedigree cats was adopted with much gusto. Here was a worthwhile hobby, having for its focal point a creature of beauty and charm – a creature that could step right into our lives and respect our way of living. Cat clubs have been the nurseries in which the show cat has been developed; almost everywhere there is a boom in them. Where formerly only regional clubs existed, now almost every small township assembles its cat-loving community to press on with the establishment of its own special cat

clubs. It has been discovered that a stimulating social life develops where cat fanciers foregather. The publication of club newsletters provides added interest. In Britain, the Cat Fancy is growing so fast that some of us find it difficult to keep in step with the enthusiasts.

One does not usually attempt to crash into the precious world of show cats unless one has served an apprenticeship as a simple cat lover. To get in with one's feet on the right rung it is important to select carefully the breed most appealing to oneself and one's family; especially is it important to have husband or

wife co-operation. This is a hobby that is so enthralling that one can hardly go it alone. It gets so deeply under one's skin that one can never isolate it from mundane human situations.

Today there are over fifty breeds from which to select. Although strictly speaking they are all of the same species, for show purposes the Governing Council of the Cat Fancy has allowed this terminology to stand. Broadly speaking show cats are divided into three main classes: Long-hair or Persian, Short-hair British, and Short-hair Foreign. In America the situation is slightly different, as described later.

The Long-hair is the most magnificent and outstanding of all cats. It has a commanding presence, and speaks of luxury and wealth. It is divided into various breed numbers, according to colour and type. Long-haired Whites are again sub-divided into three more divisions: those with blue eyes, those with orange eyes, and those with odd eyes. The Odd-eyes, only recently recognized, are not yet eligible for championships, although paradoxically they can compete for Best in Show awards. The Chinchilla, a cat of distinctive colouring, having a white undercoat

These illustrations from the well known 'Book of the Cat' by Frances Simpson show the great woman fancier judging at the Richmond Show in 1901, and two well bred short-haired cats of the same date.

and back, flanks, head and ears tipped with black, and round expressive emerald or blue-green eyes, is an old breed whose popularity has never waned.

The Blue Persian is considered by many to be the king of all cats. He is a very well-known and long-established breed. Rather larger than the white-coated Persians, at shows he looks as if he ruled the land. For many years British breeders of class have exported Blue Persians to America, where many winning Blues have British cats in their pedigrees. The Birman, a breed only recently recognized in Britain, achieved almost instant popularity. It bears a certain resemblance to the exquisite Colourpoints only in so far as both breeds have captured something from the two-tone markings of the Siamese. Other less popular Persians are Blacks, Tortoiseshells, Bi-Coloureds and Tabbies.

Ownership of Long-hairs is not for the casual or easy going; it is a cat for the industrious cat lover who takes pride in presentation. Talcum cleansing powder is used with good

A Christmas card dated 1894 which opens up (below) and shows how popular cats were in many households. This was the era when shows were first established.

effect, but must be brushed out immediately. Cats which appear at shows bearing signs of loose powder can be disqualified. It is sometimes necessary to wash a cat all over but great care should be taken to ensure that he is dried quickly. A well-cared-for Persian should have no knots in his coat.

Another newcomer to the ranks of our recognized pedigree cats is the Turkish cat, which has rather unusual markings. It is regarded as being of modified foreign type with long hair, but it must not have the round head, short nose, and small ears of the recognized Long-hair.

Among British Short-hairs the British Blue is the most outstanding. A good second is the Silver Tabby, which has a very special charm all its own. With black markings on a silver background it catches the eye at shows. Spotted Short-hairs have recently been given a breed number, and there are still too few of them seen at shows. The self-coloured Black and Whites lack the same appeal. The tail-less Manx has now been featured on the reverse of

'Fur and Feather' is the oldest publication in the cat world and is the magazine of the cat fancy; the cover in August 1890 (above) shows an 'Ideal Striped Tabby', and a photograph of two of the earliest Siamese cats to come to England.

a five shilling coin issued in the Isle of Man, an honour few cats have achieved.

Foreign Short-hairs are so called because of their difference in type to British cats. They should be long in body, not cobby or stout in build. Ears should be pricked and rather large. Eyes should be almond shaped. Heads should be long and wedge shaped, not round like the head of the British cat. Legs should be slim and tails long and tapering.

The cat that has stamped the words Foreign type indelibly into our cat vocabulary is the Siamese. A winning Siamese bears no resemblance to any other cat except to those which have tried to steal from it by breeding. It is the most distinctive of all breeds, and whatever its heritage it is no ordinary cat. Experimental breeders have added novelty by introducing new colours. By careful and selective breeding it is now possible to have many distinct colours in mask, legs and tail. The original and best known is the Seal Point. This cat must have a dark mask and the body colour

Donbank Baby Doll, six times best in show at championship shows.

Right, an adorable Chinchilla kitten with a beautiful black spangled coat.

Top left, Blue-eyed White cats are not seen so often as Orange-eyed cats, although they are the much older breed. A Blue Persian considered to be the king of all cats (below), but this ginger Persian (above) could rival any cat, particularly in the length of his whiskers . . .

Right; however used to travelling in baskets cats become, they are always glad to get out.

should be cream, fading into fawn. Contrast is essential for beauty. The fashionable Siamese cat today has a long head and body, elegant limbs, and of course the traditional oriental blue eyes. These standards are the same for all the colours.

American fanciers are today exhibiting Siamese of unusual quality. The long head and fine muzzle are well developed. Many top winning show cats have British-bred cats in their pedigree. Lilacs are sometimes called Frost Points, and Tabby-Points called Lynx. These are small differences. As in Britain, the American-bred Siamese cat has

attained a popularity never equalled by any other breed. It is the show cat *par excellence* of this generation.

Other foreign Short-hairs are Burmese and Abyssinians. These two breeds are bred in different varieties of coat colour, the Blue Burmese being officially recognized. As yet the Champagne Burmese does not have a breed number. Abyssinians, too, can be classed as either Red or Normal-coloured. Both are exciting and are well represented at shows. The Chestnut-Brown Foreign, now renamed Havana after its American counterpart has not yet achieved the high

popularity of the other foreign breeds.

The curly-coated or Rex cat is another variety which is gaining great favour among the cat lovers of Britain. Two different varieties are recognized, the Devon and Cornish, each distinctly different according to agreed standards. Early faults were a tendency to hairlessness. English varieties have been exported to America and to many other countries. Apart from their unusual appearance they are attractive in manner, being good-humoured and friendly. They are exceedingly healthy and very easy

99

to feed. Show preparation for the Short-hair is easy, as they usually keep themselves fairly trim. Nevertheless they should have a little grooming and be made familiar with the aids to beauty known to the experts.

In America, with several Governing Councils presiding over the affairs of the cat, there are differences in breed names and point allocation. We still have no Peke-faced Reds, Himalayans, Calicos, Shaded Silvers, Maine Coon Cats or Korats on our lists. Sometimes there is only a difference of a split hair between one breed and another of similar type and colouring, yet this split hair, if analyzed by experts, might establish a new breed. We are living in an age of progress and the cat has at last come into his own.

And so, as described, there are many breeds from which to select. More detailed descriptions of these and other pedigree cats are given elsewhere in this book in the chapters on the Siamese, Unusual Breeds and New Breeds. If one is undecided the easiest way is to go to a cat show and see the animals in the flesh; no printed catalogues or splendid photographs can compare with the sight of the living creature. Although one should never buy a cat at a show, one can look about and talk to the breeders in whose exhibits one is interested. An appointment can be made to go to a cattery to make a selection which can be collected at a later date. It is risky buying a valuable kitten from a show pen, as he may have picked up a germ or been upset by the crowds.

If one has weighed up all the pros and cons of keeping a show cat and finds that one has the leisure to indulge this interest, it is nice to start with a kitten, preferably a queen. Then it is advisable to join a cat club and make the acquaintance of other fanciers with tastes similar to your own. This can be the commencement of friendships that will bring lasting rewards.

It is important to remember that breeding will out, even with cats. Your first show kitten must come from good stock and if you are very lucky it may already have proved itself at a show in a kitten class. Though kittens do not always main-

tain their early promise a winning kitten has a better chance of later wins than an unproven novice. Lucky for the fancier who starts his life in the cat show world with a promising, attractive kitten!

It is not necessary to confine oneself to exhibiting breeding cats. For many reasons it may not be practical to have more than one cat about the house, in which case it may be preferable to have your kitten neutered. There are many classes for neuters and it can become a Premier and a Grand Premier. Show going with a neutered companion can be more predictable than with breeding cats! Neutering a male cat is easy. The spaying of a female is not now considered to be dangerous, and is such common practice that few veterinary surgeons have any anxiety about its outcome.

Certain preliminaries should always be adhered to when making a date for a show. The risk of infection is always present in crowded halls and a visit to your veterinary surgeon should be part of your pre-show exercise. If your kitten has not been inoculated against the killer enteritis, it must be protected by postponing its debut until all hazards to health have been eliminated. The veterinary surgeon will advise you in all these serious matters. Nothing must be allowed to diminish the thrill that will be yours at your first show.

It should be remembered that all cats need attention to their extremities, and to their eyes and ears. Fleas should never be seen in show cats, and any signs of worm infestation should not be tolerated. If the cat is the very least little bit off colour it should immediately be withdrawn from competition. A keen exhibitor will sense that all is not well, and will only give a final gloss to an exhibit already in the pink of condition.

The diet of the show cat should present no problems, but it must be varied. A diet consisting wholly of cooked meat from which all fat, gristle and bone have been removed can cause calcium and vitamin deficiencies. Constitutionally cats do not differ, so it would be to the advantage of the show cat if he

Siamese cats are possibly the most popular of all the cats at a show.

could find his own extras, hunting and foraging like the common cat.

Many cat lovers ignore the pre-show send off. A cat may be disturbed by long motor rides, especially if it is not accustomed to being confined to a basket or cat box. The sudden restraint can play havoc with its nerves, and when it is being judged it may suddenly lose its polish and gentle bearing, and be a frustrated inhibited exhibit. Sometimes the coat becomes rough and staring, and it is not unknown for cats to develop a temperature after a long journey. A keen fancier will be aware of these problems and will accustom his cat to being a fellow traveller on journeys which have a happy ending, so that when it sets off for a show it does so with joy in its heart. If it can travel loose in the car, or preferably on a lead, that is all to the good.

There are all kinds of new situations which the coming and going to shows impose on your cat. Generally it will be accommodating, but there will be times when it is not. Sometimes cats have to sleep out on the night before a show. This is not the 'sleeping out' it might prefer. It is in fact 'sleeping in', in new surroundings. Not all hotels open up willingly to cats, although if the management is agreeable then cats can be star boarders. However, it is never advisable to accept hospitality for an entire male. He has certain habits that preclude him from sharing the refinements of domesticity!

Not all cats are comfortable when judging starts. Adult cats immediately involved in breeding do not, as a rule, make good show cats. Stud cats can sometimes be difficult, especially if there are restless, calling queens in their vicinity. A keen fancier will have his diary continually before him so that, be the

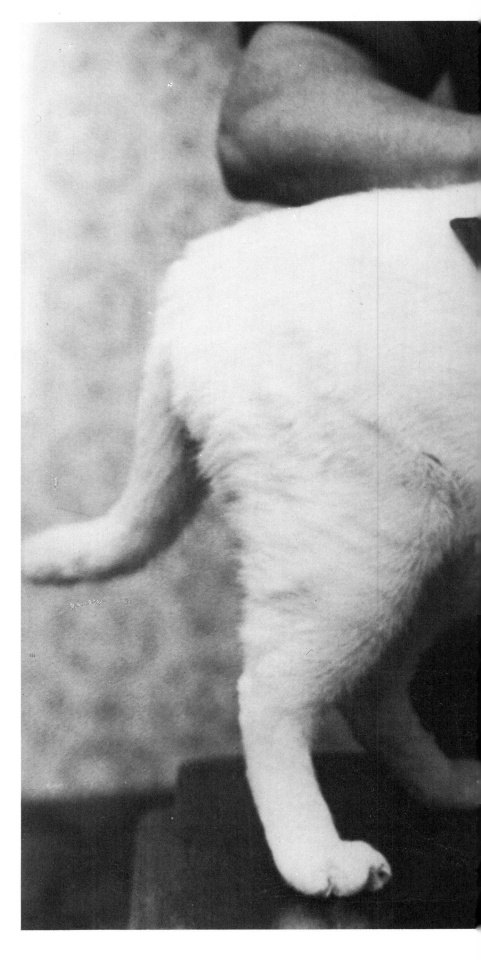

Getting ready for the show . . . a final polish with a silk handkerchief to shine up the coat.

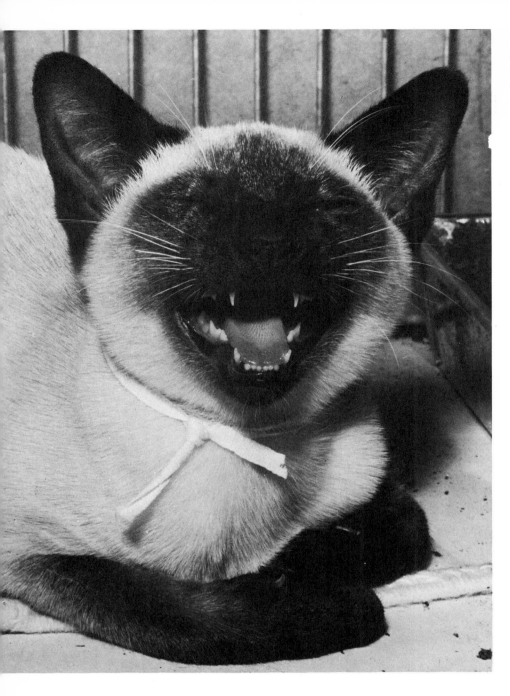

An old hand at appearing in shows just finds one more request to pose for his photograph hilariously funny . . .

Right, judging a Tabbypoint Siamese.

exhibition cat male or female, he will know which are the times most unsuitable for showing. Cats in kitten or immediately after kittening are definitely not show cats. They may have had their day, or perhaps their time is still to come.

The cat owner should enter the show hall happy in the fact that he has kept to all the rules, especially those relating to illness in the cattery. If his cat is stricken with or convalescent from any of the infectious diseases referred to on the entry form, he should not even be present. It is most unusual to find

that rules have been broken, for cat breeders are among the most honourable of all animal lovers.

Again certain procedures must be adhered to in the show hall. All cats must pass a veterinary inspection before they take their place in the numbered pens. Everything in the way of furnishings should be white. Embroidered frills or fancy blankets could bring disqualification. One blanket, under which a hot water bottle may be placed is sufficient. Cats should not be fed before judging takes place. In Britain, once the show manager has

announced that the show has started all exhibitors should leave the hall. Only at the National Show in Olympia are exhibitors and spectators permitted to be present. Once the show is in progress the exhibitors may not return to their pens except by request of the show manager. In the case of illness or disarray an exhibitor can be summoned to attend to his or her cat.

Show procedures differ in different countries. In Britain the judge and her steward take up their place in front of each pen and the cat is placed on a table for inspection. It

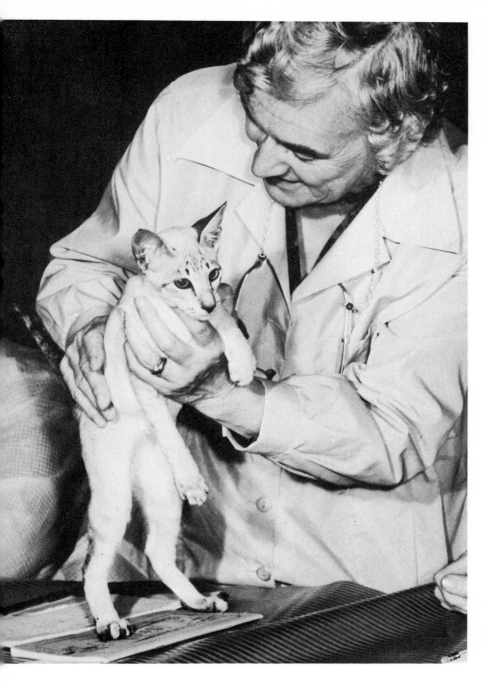

pions to win the first round of the process, and then have to repeat this success at two more shows and be first in both under different judges – all of which proves to be extremely challenging. These rules also hold good for the Grand Premier class. The American system of judging is different, allowing for extra show points scored on one occasion to bring them the honour.

The climax of a British cat show is the Best in Show judging, when nominations from open class winners are voted for, one against another. The final honours are well fought for and won, and good stewards plan this part of a show with particular attention. They are keen and interested, for they know they are to be the judges of tomorrow.

The ambition of many owners of show cats is to be able to export them, which can be very remunerative. Quarantine regulations restrict this activity somewhat, although export to America has always been easy for British breeders. All a cat needs is a veterinary certificate and various other simple documents. The cat can fly to his new home without a care in the world; can breakfast in England and arrive in a new American home for dinner. This ease of transport has helped considerably to keep the two Cat Fancys together, and also means that champions in one country can be champions in another.

The world of show cats is a world of interest and many delights. There are sorrows, too, for our beloved cats have only a brief span of life in comparison to ours. Those of you who have shared your happiest moments with special cats will appreciate what I am trying to say. When our faithful friend is suddenly bewildered by the terrifying agony that may precede death it is hard to admit that you, his God, are only human after all. You cannot help. There is a greater force over which you have no control.

The companionship of a cat is very worthwhile in a world that can be cold and hard, and the companionship of a show cat is something of real joy to a cat lover. As soon as he enters the scene he becomes your shadow and delight.

is important that the cat is relaxed and stands quietly, for it has to submit to much handling by the judge and steward. Anonymity is essential. The work of the judge is silently performed, for he has to keep his own council until the end of the show. The magic word Champion, so long eluded, may at last be within reach.

In America there is a different judging procedure, although many European countries follow the British system. There is also a slight variation between the various States in America, as they are controlled

by different governing bodies. The usual procedure is for the judge to be seated at a long table, in view of the exhibitors and spectators. The competitors' names are called out and the breeders or owners bring their cats up to the table and sit down to watch the judging. It is usual for the judge to elaborate on his findings, which must be very helpful to the novice exhibitor as well as to the established breeder.

In Britain the title of Grand Champion is most elusive, for entrants have to compete in a class of not less than seven other cham-

He is ever obedient to your call and willingly abandons his place by the fire to go with you to new scenes among cat-enchanted folk. His is not a repressed or miserable life, as show critics would have the world believe. His is an extraordinarily comforting and happy one for he loves to be with people. He is assured of a nice, warm bed wherever he goes. First-class hotels receive him as though he were a prince, and boots and butlers acclaim his beauty. His diet is the most choice and appetizing ever put before a cat. His health and well-being are everyone's concern. If his eyes water, or his nose drips, he is immediately handed out his quota of antibiotics. If he has a tummy upset even the master of the house would forego his nip of brandy if it would bring solace to the cat. He can take life easy. He has no need to plan for the future. Even his sex life is taken care of.

All things considered the show cat is a winner: so many people are interested in him. Pet foods are advertized as suitable for pedigree cats, and pet stores supply everything from a toothbrush to an electric blanket to cater for this special breed of cat. The veterinary brains of feline research bureaux are forever trying to prolong his life. At this juncture we can hang our heads in shame. The sins of our forefathers are our sins too. How little was done for the domestic cat until the show cat came into his own!

As breeder, exhibitor, show manager, secretary, president, delegate and judge, my life has been enriched by the many associations I have made. There is an affinity between cat lovers all the world over. Distance, race and colour matter little. To have found each other has given to each a new zest for living.

My first real contacts were made as a breeder and exhibitor. Contacts that were lasting because they had as their foundations the identity of one special cat. It may have been a stud cat or a breeding queen. No matter. It was he or she who brought together two people in a friendship that was rewarding to both. As secretary and show mana-ger my circle of friends was enlarged, and my knowledge of the way other cat lovers lived was increased. As president of the Northern Siamese Cat Society I could sit back and look around me as if I had a seat in the House of Lords. As delegate to the Governing Council I received an insight into the establishment. As a judge my life in the world of show cats was made. Close association with show cats was like a first glimpse of the celestial bodies.

In Britain the show cat and his progenitors have begat a new race of folk. There are so many that naming is here impossible. From America, almost written into our language, come names like Richard Gebhardt, Mrs Betty O'Brien, Mrs Ellen Dickie, Mrs Rita Swenson, Mrs Marge Naples, Mr Sam Sheer, Mrs Vera M. Nelson, Mrs Daphne Negus and our own representative on the International Committee of the Cat Fanciers' Association, Mrs Eileen Lentaigne.

Writers about pedigree cats have a special place in the heart of show cat owners. In Britain we have nothing to compare with the American *Cat Fanciers' Year Book*, edited by Christine Streetman and now in its thirteenth edition. It is superbly put together, a record of the top cats in America and of the people whose lives have been enriched by their association with class cats. The only magazine entirely devoted to cats in Britain today is *Cats*, a new publication by two well-known cat lovers Hazel and Patrick Glover. Unfortunately it is published only quarterly and might not satisfy the appetite of avid readers. Every edition carries letters of appreciation from American readers, whose love for the British cat and its ways will never diminish.

In *Fur and Feather*, the official organ of the Cat Fancy, we have the oldest publication in the cat world. In times of peace and war it has kept going our interest in show cats. Unfortunately, what was once a valuable weekly publication is now published only fortnightly.

In Britain, in recent years, an increasing number of authors have written about the show cat; names well-known in this field are Rose

Burmese cats are now very popular in America and Britain, although they were not brought over from Burma until 1930. Of Foreign type, they have a rounder face than the Siamese and are a lovely rich seal brown colour, with only slightly darker 'points'. (See the chapter on Unusual Breeds).

Tenent, Grace Pond, Phylis Lauder, Kit Wilson, Elizabeth Towe, Helen and Sidney Denham, Kathleen R. Williams, Ann L. Stubbs and last, but I hope not least, the present writer. A cat lover of interest and glamour from the publishing world is the Hon. Mrs Michael Joseph, who from constantly reading my proofs has all the standards for pedigree cats at her fingertips.

In recent years show support has come from American clubs, and we, in turn offer rosettes to American cat clubs. The premier cat club, the National, in 1970 offered specials from:

Mr R. Gebhardt (USA): Manx pin for best Manx

Mr J. Bannon (USA): Voodoo medal for best black Persian

Abyssinian Cat Club of America, through Mrs Carlton W. Pallady: rosettes for Best Champion Abyssinians, male and female

The United Burmese Cat Fanciers of USA, through Mrs C. W. Pallady: ribbons for best Brown Champion Burmese, male and female

Pet Pride Inc. of the USA, through Mrs A. Strobel: a plaque for best long-haired cat in show.

Never having lost my enthusiasm for cat shows I can look back and quote from heart from my first cat book *Cats in Clover*. My critics wrote that I was over-exuberant, my cat-loving friends simply wallowed in it:

'On receipt of my first schedule, I plunged wholeheartedly into this new wonderland of cats. I hied myself to a quiet corner and read and digested every word it contained. The telephone bell rang but I did not hear it. From that moment only one bell sounded, and it rang out cute classification, clear terminology and deep insinuations, and behind it all was the exciting knowledge that three weeks from now I would be a novice exhibitor.

'That night I filled in my first entry form, supplied the data of age, sire, dam and registration number. (1) Open Blue Point Kitten, male or female, 6–9 months. Scylla Panida. There was now no going back. I had indeed become a novice exhibitor.

'Life offers many jobs and a host of absorbing and thrilling situations from time to time, but there is no situation so ecstatic as that first day of initiation, your baptism of *fur*, when you leave behind the world of just 'cat loving' to become a somebody in the great universe of Cat Fanciers, in short, a Novice Exhibitor.

'Many are the happy days, and many the blessings I have counted since I signed my first entry form. But none can ever surpass the gratification I felt on that never-to-be-forgotten day when I walked with arms outstretched and heart laid bare into that show hall carrying my first pedigree cat.'

Above, a winning Siamese kitten is glad to be back with its owner after the ordeal of its first show.

Left, a magnificent Red Abyssinian, (known in America as the 'Sorrel' cat. These are 'one-man' cats, are highly intelligent and talk a lot – (See the chapter on New Breeds).

Kittens galore

Kittens of every kind and colour – Kittens in many different moods – kittens playing – kittens fighting . . .

. . . naughty kittens and obedient kittens — fluffy longhairs or Siamese they are all enchanting and always loveable and amusing.

The new breeds

CHRISTINE METCALF

Since ancient times the domestic cat has mated readily with its small cousins. The result of their random habits was a complexity of colour, size and structure. Some cat owners were interested in perpetuating the strains which most appealed to them. They segregated those cats showing the qualities they desired and allowed them to mate only with cats showing similar characteristics. Soon they were able to anticipate each generation breeding true so that a strain became a breed. In 1871, Harrison Weir, an artist interested in cats, conceived the idea of presenting a cat show as described in the chapter on The World of Show Cats. This first show was the forerunner of shows all over the world, and was also the beginning of the Cat Fancy in Britain.

Interest in showing cats, and in competition, spread to New York by 1895 and the following year Paris followed suit. This newly awakened interest in the beauty of breeds created a need for organization, and the participating countries began to look around them for ways of enhancing the cat. Breeders everywhere were looking for sources of good stock. Long-haired cats were brought from the East and the first Siamese cats were imported. Planned breeding with records of the cats' names was the beginning of the pedigree, and people interested in different varieties of cats formed clubs to promote interest in them. At this time Harrison Weir produced a list of attributes to aim for. His *Points of Excellence* was used as a basis for the standards set by the first registering body.

In 1910 the Governing Council of the Cat Fancy was formed, composed of delegates from the various affiliated clubs and societies, which today generally controls cat breeding in Britain. In the United States the American Cat Fanciers' Association plays a similar role. Many of the breeds acceptable to both associations are original entrants but many new breeds have been added to the lists over the years. Although it is only a century since breeding records were first kept there are today more than fifty different

A sparkling Tabby Cameo Cat with beautiful markings. They are very popular in America though they are not yet recognized by the Cat Fancy in Britain.

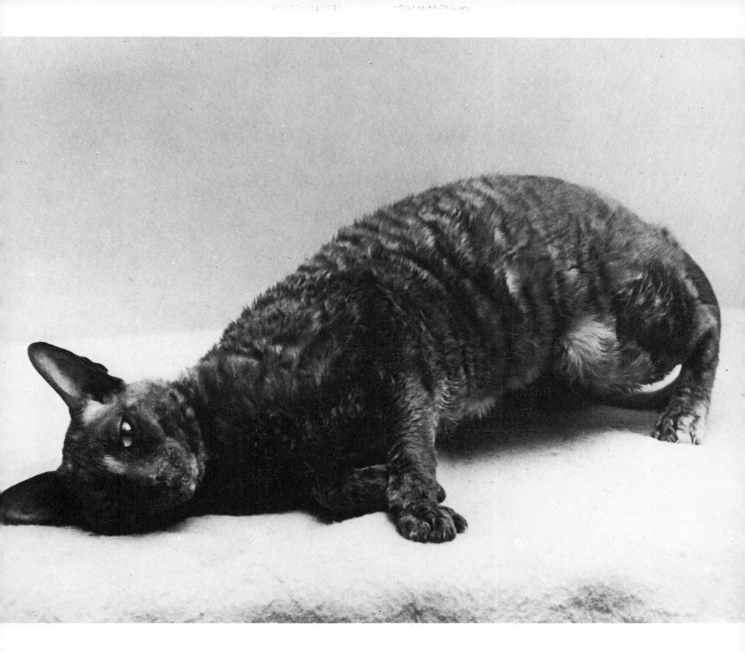

varieties of beautiful pedigree cats.

In 1950, on a farm in Cornwall, a very peculiar kitten appeared in a litter born to a pair of farm cats, a Tortoiseshell mother and an unknown father. The kitten was peculiar because it had a curly coat – normally cats have straight hair whether it be long or short. This kitten was recognized by the owner as being unique, and in order to reproduce the mutant gene it was eventually mated back with the mother. The result was more curly kittens; in fact 50% of the litter had this strange, short, silky coat. The hair on the body was much shorter than that of a normal short coat and each individual hair was waved. No guard hairs were visible because

they were shortened to just below the level of the top coat. Even the whiskers and eyebrows were crinkled. It is not known what produced this mutation but geneticists believe it involved a single recessive factor.

Less than 10 years after the appearance of Cornish Rex-coated Cat Gene One, as it was called, a curly coated kitten appeared in a litter in Devon. It was presumed there was a connection between the two and cross-matings were arranged, without success. The resulting kittens all had straight hair, which showed that the Devon and the Cornish were caused by two different genes and accordingly the second cat became known as the

A curly-coated Rex cat.

Left, a brown Burmese – it is not difficult to see why this cat was regarded as sacred in Burma.

Devon Rex-coated Cat Gene Two. There is a slight variation between them in that the Cornish cat usually has a thicker coat than the Devon.

Curiously, at about the same time as the Rex cat appeared in Britain, the same mutant was reported in Germany but it did not breed true, and in the United States a litter of curly coated cats was unfortunately destroyed. However, British bred cats have been exported to America and are now an established breed. This hair type can be transferred to any breed, colour or type of cat, and curly coated cats have now received official recognition on both sides of the Atlantic.

The standards for the Devon Rex and the Cornish Rex-coated Cats are very similar; both have long slender bodies and are medium in size, hard and muscular. Their legs should be long and fine, giving an overall impression of being high on the legs, and with small, oval paws. The tails of both are long, fine and whiplike; the neck should be slender. The head of the Cornish should have a straight profile, that of the Devon should have a nose with a definite stop, giving it a Roman profile. Disqualification occurs in America for coarse or guard hairs. The British judges fault the

The other kind of curly-coated cat comes from Devon and differs from the Cornish cat in having a slightly thinner coat and a roman profile.

Right, the Havana or Chestnut-Brown is a cross between a black Long-hair and a Siamese, and is an example of a man-made breed.

Rex-coated Cat for white mismarkings. Any coat colour or pattern is permitted.

The Governing Council of the Cat Fancy will not allocate a breed number, that is it will not recognize a standard, until a new breed can be bred true. There must also be enough fanciers interested in a new variety to justify registration. It took many years of selective breeding to produce the Chestnut-Brown, which was once known in Britain as the Havana until the name was dropped to avoid wild stories being invented about its origin. In the United States the breed is still known by this name, although the cat is a product of British breeders, an example of a man-made breed.

It occurred in the first place because a Black Long-hair female mismated with a Seal Point Siamese. One of the black female kittens born as a result was again mated with a Siamese, and one of the litter carried the chocolate gene of the Siamese. It was an all-brown male, differing from the Burmese in the shape of its body. The Chestnut-Brown closely resembles the Russian Blue in type and it is a warmer colour than the Burmese, being a rich, warm, mahogany brown all over.

In Britain the Governing Council state that the eyes should be slanting and oriental in shape. In America the Cat Fanciers' Association requires that the eyes should be chartreuse green, oval in shape and set almost straight. The head should be set on a graceful, but not long, neck, and the head should be longer than its width, with ears set wider apart than the Siamese, and pricked forward. The Americans describe it as having a 'pixie look'. Chestnut-Brown Cats are of the foreign type, they are fine in bone, lithe, sinuous and of graceful proportions, and should never be heavy. Any shade of chestnut brown is acceptable. The short, glossy coat may show no shadow points, as may be seen occasionally in the Burmese. Kittens frequently show tabby 'ghost' markings when changing coat, but this should never be held against an otherwise good kitten.

All Short-haired breeds belong to one of two distinct body types, the one exception being the Manx Cat as described in the chapter on Unusual Breeds. They are either British Short-hairs or Foreign Short-hairs. The body of the British Short-hair should be distinguishable by its well-knit and powerful frame. It should have good depth with a

full, broad chest. The tail should be thick at the base and well set, with its length in proportion to its body. The legs should be strong and well proportioned with neat, well-rounded feet. The head should be broad between the ears, the cheeks well developed, and the face and nose short. The British-type cat is a sturdy looking animal.

In contrast the Foreign Short-hair should be lightly built, long and lissom. The head should be long and wedge shaped, wide at the top and narrowing to a fine muzzle. The eyes should be almond shaped and the ears large, being wide at the base, pointed and pricked. Keeping the proportions balanced with the head, neck and ears, the long svelte body and the fine legs and feet, the tail should be thin and whipped, tapering to a point at the top.

A cat not yet recognized by the Cat Fanciers' Association in America

is the Blue Burmese. The Brown Burmese is an old favourite and was imported to Britain from America in 1947, when it was found that from some of these strains a number of cats with blue coats were appearing. This colour was greatly admired and breeders set about producing a true strain. Colour is the only difference between the Blue and the Brown Burmese, and that for the Brown should be solid, rich, dark seal brown, shading to slightly lighter on chest and belly. There should be no white or tabby markings. The ears, mask and points should be only slightly darker than the back coat colour. The body of the Blue Burmese adult cat should be predominantly bluish-grey, darker on the back and the over-all effect being a warm colour, with a silver sheen to the coat. The ears, mask and points should shade to silver grey.

The Blue Burmese differs from the Brown Burmese only in the colour of its coat, which is a bluish-grey with a silver sheen.

Right, a really elegant Foreign White showing all the features of these cats; the pointed face, large ears and almond shaped eyes; oval paws, lissom body and long, tapering tail.

Most pedigree cats have been introduced to the rest of the world from Britain, but the Burmese is an exception, a Brown Burmese having initially been taken from India to the United States in 1930. The breed has been known for centuries in Burma, where at one time they were raised in the temples and regarded as sacred; but they are comparative newcomers to the Western world. It was from the cat imported to America that all pure-bred Burmese were eventually produced.

The Burmese is a Foreign type cat which differs from its Siamese cousin on many points. Its body is not so long, its head is a short, wedge shape and it is rounder. The ears should be pricked, relatively large and wide at the base. Eyes must be almond shaped and slanting towards the nose in true oriental fashion, and should be a clear golden yellow. The eye colour often causes difficulty and many Burmese have eyes of chartreuse yellow; blue eyes and squints are inadmissible. Burmese must never be fat. They make good pets because they are very affectionate, although they are volatile and have changeable temperaments.

Only recently recognized as a registered breed in Britain, and not yet given official recognition in America, is the French Birman Cat, otherwise called The Sacred Cat of Burma. There is a fascinating legend told about this breed: it is said that many years before Buddha, an old priest who had a white cat lived in the mountains of Indo-China. One day, when the man lay dying in front of a golden statue of a goddess with sapphire eyes, the cat jumped on to the throne. As the man died his soul passed into the cat. The cat's fur assumed the golden colour of the statue, and its yellow eyes became sapphire blue. The only unchanged parts were the tips of its paws which were touching its dead master's head. Less romantic but more probable than this legend is the story that the cat originated through a white footed Siamese mating with a Long-hair. There are conflicting stories about this cat being the one that was kept in great luxury by the priests in the temples in Burma. The priests believed that when they died their soul would enter the body of one of the cats, where it would reside until the death of the cat whereupon the

soul of the priest would enter paradise.

The colouring of the French Birman is the same as of the Siamese, that is seal or blue; but the face, tail and paws are dark brown with the Seals and blue-grey with the Blues. The beige of the coat is slightly golden. The paws should look as if the cat is wearing little white gloves, those on the back legs extending upwards to a point at the back of the foot. The body should be long and the legs low with short, strong paws. The head should be wide and round, but with full cheeks. The fur should be long, with a good full ruff, of a silky texture and slightly curled on the belly. The tail should be a little longer than that of the Colourpoint, and it should be bushy. The eyes should be a bright, china blue. Kittens are lighter in colour at birth, but as they grow their colour darkens.

The Colourpoint Long-hair is another of the more recent breeds to receive recognition from the Governing Council of the Cat Fancy. Each year it is becoming more and more popular, breeders in several countries having experimented over a long period with various crossings in an attempt to obtain a Long-haired Siamese. Experiments took place in the United States up until the Second World War when interest dwindled even though breeders were able to produce a cat of this type. The problem was that the slim, elegant shape of the Siamese looked less attractive with long hair.

In Britain the experiments continued, the aim being to transfer the delicate Siamese colouring and at the same time to eliminate the Siamese type. The new Long-haired Siamese produced as a result of the experiments were mated to the best possible Persians in order to obtain the Persian body shape. The result was the Colourpoint.

Even today the eyes present difficulties; the ideal specimen carries the lovely sapphire-blue eyes of a Siamese, combined with the large, round shape of a Persian. Unfortunately many Colourpoints tend to have pale blue eyes. Any similarity in type between this cat and the Siamese is now considered to be most undesirable and incorrect. The

body must be cobby and low on the legs, the head broad and round, with width between the ears. The face and nose must be short, and the tail short and full. Whilst a small kink may be permitted in the tail of a Siamese, it is most definitely a fault in a Colourpoint. The lovely Siamese colouring has been transferred to the long, thick, soft fur of the Persian. It may be seal, lilac, blue or chocolate pointed, with appropriate body colour as for the Siamese – that is, cream, glacial white, ivory or magnolia respectively. Points must be of solid colour and body shading, if any, must tone with the points.

The Himalayan Cat of the United States is basically the same as the British Colourpoint. It is a Persian cat to which the Siamese colour pattern has been transferred, and the standard for the breed is the same as for the Persian. The Colourpoint is recognized in Britain in only four of the Siamese colourings, whereas in America there are breed numbers for the Himalayan in two more, the Red Point and the Frost Point. The American Cat Fanciers' Association say the Himalayan must be firm in flesh but not fat, well balanced physically and temperamentally, gentle and amenable to handling, medium to large in size, heavily boned, short coupled, broad through the chest and rump and with short sturdy legs, giving the impression of robust power.

The next cat to be considered is taking its bow for the second time. In the early days of cat shows, cats with two distinctive colours were not unusual, but difficulty in obtaining cats without tabby markings in the self-coloured parts was found and frequently challenge certificates were withheld. Now Bi-coloured Cats are back at the shows where

A large litter of French Birman kittens, which are rather like long-haired Siamese cats with white socks on. Their colour darkens as they grow older, particularly on the face and paws.

they have received recognition for a second time, both as Long-hairs and as Short-hairs.

The colours for the standard may be black, blue, orange or cream, all with white as the second colour. The colours must be quite distinct from each other and the pattern should resemble the markings on a Dutch rabbit. The eyes may be copper, orange or amber.

The standard for the Bi-coloured Long-hair is the same as for all Long-hairs, and the Bi-coloured Short-hair has points awarded according to the standard laid down for all British Short-hairs. In all Bi-coloured cats the black, blue, orange, or cream markings should start immediately behind the shoulders round the barrel of the body, including the tail and hind legs but leaving the hind feet white. The ears and mask of the face should be self-coloured. The shoulders

should be white, as should the neck, forelegs and feet, chin, lips and blaze up the face and over the top of the head, which joins or runs into the white at the back of the skull, thus dividing the mask exactly in half. Breeding a cat with such precise colour definitions is not easy and for this reason not many are to be seen. Bi-coloured males are often chosen as mates for Tortoiseshell females.

The Abyssinian Cat is no newcomer to the show, and was first seen in England as long ago as 1869 although there seem to be conflicting opinions about the animal's origins. It is said with authority that there was no native breed in Abyssinia, but one thing is known – the first Abyssinian in the Western world was brought to Britain from that country by the wife of a British army officer. However, there are no cats answering to the description

of Abyssinians in that country to-day, so the origin remains a mystery.

Since the breed was first recognized kittens have been born from time to time that have differed in colour from all the rest – they were red. At first these caused difficulties for their breeders, who were barred from entering an otherwise fine kitten because the standard did not fit the breed. As more and more kittens with red coats appeared they became recognized as a separate variety and were eventually given a breed number. Today the Red Abyssinian is a breed in its own right, in type it is a Foreign Short-hair. The colour should be a rich copper-red with hair doubly, or preferably trebly, ticked with darker colours. Lack of distinct contrast in the ticking is considered a fault, as is a pale body colour. The eyes should be large, bright and expressive green, yellow or hazel. Normally the pads of a cat with a ruddy brown coat are black, but those of the Red Abyssinian are pink. In the United States this cat is known as the 'Sorrel'.

Two more newcomers to the scene are the Foreign White and the Foreign Lilac, whose names perfectly describe the breeds, which are self-coloured of Foreign type. The oriental shaped eyes may be golden-yellow or bright blue. Although there is a proposed standard for the white cat, a breed class has not yet been awarded. Similarly the Foreign Lilac has no set standard. Anyone interested in showing these cats would enter them in the class for Any Other Variety (in Britain) or Any Other Color (in

A Burmese cat.

Right, a Chinchilla cat.

*A Red Point Siamese kitten –
Siamese with this colouring were one
of the latest to be recognized by the
Governing Council of the Cat
Fancy, together with the Tabbypoint
and Tortie Point. Not yet as popular
as the Seal, Blue and Lilac Points,
they are, however, just as attractive.*

America), both of which classifications are for cats of any colour or pattern not specifically provided for. The cats may appear in the pedigree section of a show but they cannot compete for challenging certificates and, until the colour has been recognized for this purpose, they cannot become champions.

A cat that appeared long ago in the last century is the Chinchilla. It is not a new variety, as is sometimes supposed, and is undoubtedly one of the loveliest of all cats. The Chinchilla's beauty lies in its colouring; it must appear ethereal and there should never be any suggestion of coarseness. The breed is said to have originated from a crossing of Tortoiseshell with Silver Tabby, and this ancestry can be seen in the kittens for they are always born with tabby rings on the tail and with faint tabby markings. As they grow the markings gradually disappear and the mature cat has a pure white undercoat, each hair tipped with black to give a sparkling silver appearance. This tipping should be evenly distributed over the shoulders, back, head, flanks and tail.

Some Chinchillas, more heavily ticked than others, were known as Shaded Silver, but difficulty in distinguishing the Chinchilla from the Shaded Silver, when the ticking of one was light and the other heavy, caused the class to be withdrawn in Britain. In America and on the Continent it is still a recognized breed. The undercoat of the Silver is more grey than white; where the Chinchilla is silver, the Shaded Silver looks more like pewter.

The Masked Silver resembles the Silver except for the face which is masked with very dark colour; the paws, also, are dark. The eyes of these cats may be emerald or blue-

A beautiful Spotted Red cat.

Right, a Blue Colourpoint Long-hair and a Seal Colourpoint Long-hair; and below, Seal Colourpoint kittens. These are Persian type cats with Siamese colouring and are becoming increasingly popular.

Left, a Red Abyssinian.

Right, a Shell Cameo cat.

Bottom, a Foreign Lilac, which is like the Foreign White only a greyish-blue in colour. Neither of these cats is yet recognized in America or Britain by the Cat Fancies.

green in colour, and the nose tip should be bright red. The type is as for all Long-hairs but the cat's build should be lighter to accentuate the fairy-like quality.

The Cameo Cats, recognized by the American Cat Fanciers' Association, are among the newest of the breeds and are not yet recognized by the Governing Council of the Cat Fancy in Britain. There are four Cameos, and they must conform to the general standards of the regular Persian. The pattern is the same as that for Silvers. Their colour, a combination of cream and red, has been developed intensively over a period of twenty years in America, where they have now become very popular.

In the Shell Cameo the undercoat should be pale cream, almost white. The hair on the back, flank, head and tail should be sufficiently tipped with red to give a delicate tinsel appearance; the face and legs may be very slightly shaded with tipping but the chin, ear tufts, stomach and chest should be the pale colour without tipping. The Shaded Cameo has red tipping that is considerably heavier than that of the Shell and gives the cat a positively hot glow, although the colour diminishes gradually into the sides to meet the ivory-white of the underside. The Smoke Cameo should be a deep-reddish-beige with a white or well contrasted cream undercoat, red or deep beige points, and mask with white or pale cream neck ruff and ear tufts. No tabby markings or brown tinge are permitted. Eyes should be gold or copper, the eye rims and nose leather should be

rose. The fourth member of the Cameo group is the Tabby Cameo, whose ground colour of pale cream should be broken with well defined red or beige tabby markings. Like the Chinchillas and the Silvers, the over-all effect should be light and sparkling.

Spotted Cats are as old as time. Long ago, when the name of every family had a symbolic meaning, the English Catesby family adopted a spotted cat for their sign. The Catesby crest, bearing the cat, can be seen on a stained glass window in Lapworth Church, Warwickshire. Why then are these among the newest entrants at the shows when they are the oldest cats known?

Many of our wild cats bear a wide variety of spots; there are large spots and small spots, many and few. The spots may differ in shape, some being oblong or round, others even rosette shaped. In a pedigree cat, however, the spots may be placed or shaped, the important factor is that they must be clear and distinct, not merging into one another. The colour of the spots must contrast well with the background, which may be of any colour. The whole body should be spotted, and stripes and bars are considered a fault, except on the face and head. The

standards for the Spotted Cat are as for all British Short-hairs. Early in the century a number of them were to be seen at the shows, but for some reason the pedigree died out. Like the Bi-coloured Cat it is now making a second appearance, and in rapidly increasing numbers.

Perhaps the most popular of all the British Short-hairs is the British Blue, which is an impressive, sturdy framed animal, for its colour is now a lovely lavender blue, making a beautiful contrast with the lustrous amber eyes. The British Blue is not a new breed but its colour has been improved from the former dark slate or plum blue. The texture of the coat is important in a specimen cat, and should be short and soft, never harsh to the touch. The standards for the British Blue are as for all Short-hairs in Britain. This breed is seldom seen in the United States although they are so popular in Britain that there is often a waiting list for kittens.

There is a French breed very similar to the British Blue, called the Chartreux, the standard for which requires any shade of grey, or greyish-blue.

The very latest Siamese cats to receive recognition by the Governing Council of the Cat Fancy in

Britain are the Tabbypoint, Red Point and Tortie Point. Tabby markings appear regularly in all breeds of cats because the gene for tabby is dominant and for this reason is difficult to breed out. Because it is so persistent it often causes an otherwise good cat to lose points at shows. Recently breeders discovered that they can produce these markings as required, and a carefully planned breeding programme has transferred the pattern to the points of the Siamese. The Tabbypoint is typically Siamese in type, with tabby markings on the mask, especially round the nose, eyes and cheeks, which should be clearly defined; the whisker pads should be darkly spotted. The legs

should bear broken stripes of varying size but there should be solid markings on the back of the hind legs. The tail should be ringed, ending in a solid tip. The ears, too, should be in solid colour without stripes, and the colour should look rather like a thumb print.

The Red Point has a body colour of white, shading to apricot on the back. Its points are bright, reddish gold.

The body of the Tortie Point should be cream or fawn with shading to match the basic colour of the points, to which the tortoiseshell colouring is restricted. The ears may be Seal sprinkled with red, or red sprinkled with Seal. The mask should have the Seal and

cream patches in equal proportions; traces of red are permissible but evenness of patching is not essential. The legs and feet should be marbled with red or ivory, or both. As with all Tortoiseshell cats, Tortie Points are mostly females.

A few years ago a pair of cats were imported to Britain from Turkey. The owner mated them and the resulting kittens bred true. The Turkish Cat has very recently received a breed number from the Governing Council of the Cat Fancy in Britain and is a very beautiful cat, most elegant with its long flowing coat, so soft and silky. The ground colour is white, with markings of a rich auburn colour, and head and tail ringed in light and dark shades.